SETTLEMENT OF PENDLETON DISTRICT

1777 - 1800

By

Frederick Van Clayton

Please direct all correspondence and orders to:

www.southernhistoricalpress.com
or
SOUTHERN HISTORICAL PRESS, Inc.
PO BOX 1267
375 West Broad Street
Greenville, SC   29601
southernhistoricalpress@gmail.com

ISBN #0-89308-639-8

Printed in the United States of America

Dedicated To

Anne Sheriff
who indexed and arranged for its publication

Miss Faith Clayton
who donated the manuscript from her collection
and assisted Van, her brother, in his research endeavors

Julia Woodson
who is always there when needed

Morris Clayton
who is Van's son
and gave permission to published his father's thesis

Frederick C. Holder
who wrote the introduction.

Frederick Van Clayton

Frederick Van Clayton was born August 19, 1893 in Central, South Carolina. He was the second son of Dr. Lawrence G. Clayton and Addie Smith Clayton. He graduated from Central Wesleyan College and the University of South Carolina where he received a Master of Arts degree in history and served as associate professor of history.

Mr. Clayton was a former superintendent of Easley and Pickens High School. He coached the first football team that Pickens High ever produced. Then he served as Superintendent of Education in Pickens County before and after World War I. He was a veteran of World War I serving in the U. S. Navy and was owner and editor of the Pickens Sentinel in the twenties.

As one of the county's leading historians, he organized and served as first President of Pickens County Historical Society. He married Inez Morris and they had one son Robert Morris Clayton.

Frederick Van Clayton was both a product and an active participant of the rural south. As part owner of a funeral home in Pickens, South Carolina, he developed a knowledge of the land and people that will perhaps never be equalled. In a day when roads were poor and practically non-existent in western South Carolina, the local funeral hearses did double duty as ambulances. In addition, burials were often in remote areas only accessible by a horse-drawn cart and walking mourners. A typical call for ambulance service years ago might have indicated that they lived past John Chapman's home near McKinney Chapel. Such directions were adequate at a time when place names had attained a high degree of local perfection and the person making the call was known to the receiver. Mr. Clayton had to perform the functions of a physician, minister, as well as funeral director.

Over the years, Van Clayton developed a repertoire of sayings, experiences, and tall-tales that made him an extraordinary storyteller. Unfortunately only a few have continued as part of a dying oral tradition. Instead, he recorded information regarding the history of the area from the people and area he served. This was not a late found interest, for as the following work attests, he knew more of the area before he began his business life than presumably anyone else then living.

After finding approximately ninty-five percent of all the land grants then available in the Pendleton District up to 1800, he was able to locate the majority of them on maps. Only a person with the innate knowledge that Mr. Clayton possessed regarding the area could ever have hoped to accomplish such a feat. The materials which were available to him at the time were not housed in the facilities of the Archives and Caroliniana which we find today, nor did he have the advantage of computerized indexes; however, he did have the advantage of working with a group of people in Columbia who had an intimate working knowledge of the resources which their buildings contained. Even so, the work was his own, and at the time it was completed in the late 1920's, it was a pioneering effort in the use of archival materials revealing the history of an area inland from Charleston.

It should be remembered that this book was prepared as part of the requirements for the completion of master's degree and not as a full historical study of the region. Some of the people receiving land grants never settled the land while others "stopped" for a while on their way west.

Van Clayton's work remains the most useful reference available on the early settlement of the Pendleton District. For this reason alone the text and body of work will be printed as originally written. The crux of his work remains, after over 50 years, useful to both the historical and genealogical researcher, and a landmark of research in the history of the upcountry of South Carolina.

TABLE OF CONTENTS

THE SETTLEMENT

OF

PENDLETON DISTRICT

1777-1800

By

Frederick Van Clayton

A Thesis submitted to the Department of History
of the University of South Carolina in partial
fulfillment of the requirements for the degree
of Master of Arts.

Approved By:

R S Merryweather
Major Professor

Ree T Smith
Dean of Graduate School

INTRODUCTION

The old Pendleton District, carved out of Ninety Six, was in the extreme northwestern part of South Carolina. It embraced the present counties of Anderson, Oconee, and Pickens. During its existence it was the third largest district in the State. The average length from northwest to northeast was fifty-one miles, and from northwest to southwest it was thirty-six. It contained about 1,175,004 acres.[1]

The drainage of the region is in two directions. The waters of the central and western part flow into the Savannah River, following the general direction of south and southwest. The extreme eastern part is drained by the Saluda, the streams flowing south and southeast.

The topography of the district is in general rolling. The altitude ranges from about 750 feet in the lower part of the district[2] to 3436 feet in the extreme northern part.[3] This last elevation is that of Mount Pinnacle, in the present county of Pickens, and is the highest point in South Carolina. In the northeastern portion, the northern part of Pickens County today, the chief heights are Table Rock, Mount Pinnacle, and Sassafras Mountains. Those of lesser importance, and further south, are Six Mile, Glassy, and Potato Hill mountains. In the northwestern part of the district, known as Oconee County, the land in the lower part is hilly, while that in the upper terminates in the rugged Blue Ridge Mountains. The southern part of the district, called Anderson County today, is quite rolling. The only abrupt feature is Little Mountain, near the center of the county, which rises only a few hundred feet above the surrounding county.[4]

The climate of the district might be described as mild and pleasant, and permits a variety of crops. In 1907 officials of Clemson College compiled a table of the average climactic conditions of the district, which is given below.[5]

Temperature
Mean - 60
Absolute Maximum - 102
Absolute Minimum - -7

Precipitation
Mean - 51.2
Total Amt. Driest yr. - 40.7
Total Amt. Wettest yr. - 70.2
Snow Average - 4.2

The soils of Pendleton District are of two groups, alluvial and residual. The former is rare while the latter includes all of the uplands.[6] The soils are further classified into the Cecil sandy loam, Cecil clay, Meadow, Durham sandy loam, Porter's loam, and numerous others. Of these the Cecil sandy loam and the Meadow predominate. In the Anderson section the Cecil sandy loam is 55 per cent of the total for all soils.[7] In the Oconee area it is 42.5 per cent.[8] In the Pickens section this soil is in about the same proportion.[9]

A description of the Cecil sandy loam is important since it constitutes a majority of all soils in the district. It is from four to eight inches deep and brownish-gray in color. Angular quartz fragments are found, but not in sufficient quantities to prevent cultivation of the land. Beneath this soils is found a red clay extending to a depth of several feet, the upper layer crumbles readily, while the lower part becomes heavy and compact.

The Cecil sandy loam is very desirable for general farming purposes and is capable of producing miscellaneous crops. However, cotton and corn are the principal crops grown. Due to the nature of the soil this district could be well adapted to the growing of fruits.[11]

The Meadow soils are also productive and were used almost exclusively by the early settlers. As the timber lands were cleared these soils which were found mostly in the valleys, were continually submerged and became comparatively useless.[12]

Previous to 1777 there resided in this territory the Cherokee Indians. They belonged to the Iroquoin family but were not connected very closely with the northern group. The Cherokee men were tall, slender, and erect, having a rather delicate frame. They also possessed much grace and dignity. Most of them were six feet tall and over, yet there were exceptions, Attakulkulla being a notable one. The women were short and their hands and feet were very small, but they were well formed. They were also very timid and bashful.[13]

Their general disposition was that of gravity and dignity. They were slow of speech, and very frank.[14] As a general rule the Cherokees were lazy. They were "ordinary hunters and less warrious."[15] One of their outstanding traits was a tenacious desire for their rights against encroachment of their territory.

The Cherokees were the most civilized of the southern Indian tribes. This is evidenced by their manner of living. Their houses were oblong, four square buildings, one story high. They were made of logs notched at the end and fixed one upon the other. Within, the walls were well plastered with clay tempered with grass. The roof was made of chestnut bark and sometimes long board shingles were used. The building had three apartments, with doors connecting from the inside. Close by each house was a smaller one of conical shape, called the Winter or Hot-house. It was only a few yards from the mansion house, and stood opposite the front door.[17]

The council house was built somewhat similarly to the dwellings, yet much longer, and could accommodate several hundred. It was placed upon an artificial mound, the origin of which is unknown. The inside of the building had, to some extent, the appearance of a theatre, and it was here that their councils were held. It was also used as a place of entertainment.[18]

The exact number of Indians living in what later became Pendleton District is not definitely known. In 1775 Richard Pearis furnished William Henry Drayton with an estimate of the Cherokee warriors of the lower towns. They constituted the smallest part of the nation, being practically one fourth less in number than the Overhill and Middle settlements.[19]

LOWER TOWNS	MEN
Eastatoe	40
Qualache	30
Toxaway	51
Sugar Town	29
Socauny	26
Essenneca	80
Cheowee	29
Tugelow	30
Little Chota	41
Total	356

On many occasions the Cherokees gave South Carolina trouble.

As suggested by Bartram, one of the real causes of many such troubles was the Indian trait of suspicion of the white man as he encroached upon the land. With this as a background it was an easy matter to find some immediate cause for conflict. From 1750 to 1776 there occured a number of Indian disturbances, but the two major ones were the Cherokee War of 1759 to 1761, and the uprising of 1776. The advance of settlement into the wilds of South Carolina did encroach upon the lands of the Indians, pushing them farther and farther back. The first contact as far as ultimate settlement was affected, was made by the early traders to the Indians. They brought back to the colonists a knowledge of the fertility of the country, resulting in a drift of immigration in that direction.

The Indian trade was used by the Province for a three – fold purpose, personal gain, colonial expansion, and thwarting the plans of the Spanish and French. As a result of this policy the Indians were held on friendly terms with the Province, binding them more closely to England, and the aggressions of the Spanish and French were foiled.[20] The trade was very profitable for those engaged in it and likewise served the purpose of the Province by encouraging expansion.[21] In 1751 new rules were made for the Indian trade, which were stricter than formerly. These rules regulated the employment and discharging of men, the rum question, and the amount of bond under which each trader was placed. Penalties were also provided for those violating these regulations.[22] In 1752 the Cherokee Nation had been mapped into thirteen hunting ranges and traders were assigned to each. Over one of these ranges was Cornelius Dougherty who had his house in the Indian town of Tugaloo, and was said to be one among the oldest traders to the Cherokees. He expected, if the season was fairly favorable, to collect 14,000 buckskin leathers, which in our present day money would amount to approximately $62,500.00.[23]

In 1750 there were many traders among the Cherokees. They were not only traders; in a sense they were the first settlers. During this early period there were, trading with the Cherokees, John McCord, Robert Gowdy, John Kelley,[24] Bryan Salamon, Anthony Lantague, Richard Smith, James May, Robert Emory, David McDonald, John Hatton, James Beamer, William Bates, and John Hook.[25] From among the licenses for Indian traders issued at Charleston are found such names as Dougherty, McKinney, McCormack, Millikin, and McBain.[26] The Council Journals also give Lodrick Grant, David

McDowd, William McTier, John Wat, John Downing, William McDowel, Bernard Hughes, Samuel Benn, Anthony Dean, Ambrose Davis, and James Cordridge.[27] Many of these traders were servants whose terms of indenture had expired. Their conduct among the Indians was not always above reproach, for they were noted for their "Lewdness and Wickedness," being immoral and unjust in their daily lives.[28]

The path used by these traders from Charleston to the Indian Territory is known as the Cherokee Path. It followed the watersheds of the streams which made it easily traveled.[29] From Charleston it led to the Congarees, thence to Ninety Six, and on to the headwaters of the Savannah River. From this path others led off to various places. Near the present town of Honea Path, the Cherokee Path divided, one going on to Keowee and the other to the lower towns on the Tugaloo River.[30]

The first serious war the South Carolinians had with the Indians after the Yemassee War, was that of 1759 to 1761 known as the Cherokee War. England and France after 1754 realized that one of the things necessary for their success in the war was the cultivation of the friendship of the Indians. As a result, they each began the building of forts. Governor Glen, being convinced of the necessity of protecting both frontiersmen and Indians, built Fort Prince George in 1753.[31]

After the defeat of the French during the first years of the war they renewed their efforts among the Indians and the frontiers of Pennsylvania, Virginia, and the Carolinas became the scene of action. Another cause of the Cherokee outbreak in South Carolina was the desire of the Indians to avenge a wrong they felt had been given them. It will be remembered that the Cherokees were assisting the English against the French, and on returning to their homes in the Carolinas, they stole several horses. To avenge this theft the whites, whom the Indians had been assisting, killed twelve or fourteen of their braves. The Indians on arriving home told the story in highly colored language, and aroused the nation to war.[32]

The officer at Fort Prince George advised Governor Lyttleton at Charleston of the Indian outbreak. The Governor ordered the assembling of the militia at the Congarees. In the meantime several of the Indian Chieftains made a visit to Charleston asking for peace. The Governor refused it and, making the Indians prisoners, set out for the Indian country. His "army" was in no condition to fight, and realizing his precarious condition, he decided to treat with the Indians for peace. Calling Attakulkulla, he laid before him the status of affairs. He demanded that twenty four men be given up by the Indians as hostages, which would avenge the recent outrages. Attakulkulla consented to this, but was unable to deliver the twenty four agreed upon. Despite this, Governor Lyttleton made peace and returned to Charleston.[33]

Occonostota, one of the Indian chiefs whom Governor Lyttleton had made a prisoner, longed for revenge. After a few days, he decoyed Ensign Coytomore from Fort Prince George and treacherously killed him. This caused retaliation by the force within the fort, and the Indians were again on the warpath.[34] The Indians rushed down upon the frontiers, and it was in this massacre that the Calhouns were killed.[35]

General Amherst, who was commanding in Canada, sent 1200 men under Colonel Montgomery to the aid of South Carolina. Landing in Charleston he proceeded to Monk's Corner and from there to the Congarees. Thence he marched into the Cherokee Nation destroying first the town of Eastatoe. After this he ordered his infantry to proceed against Keowee and put every male Indian to the sword. Practically all of the lower Indian towns were destroyed by Montgomery.[36]

He then started for the middle and overhill settlements in order to relieve the garrison at Fort Loudon which was being beseiged by the Indians. As he approached the Unacaye Mountains he was ambushed by the Indians at Echota near the Unacoi Gap. Although the battle was not a decisive victory, Montgomery realized that he was in danger and during the night he turned back toward Fort Prince George, gaining a day's march on the Indians. While Colonel Montgomery was successful against the Indians in the lower settlements, yet as far as breaking the power of the Cherokee Nation was concerned, he had failed.[37] The major portion of this campaign was made in the present counties of Anderson, Oconee, and Pickens.

Hardly had Colonel Montgomery returned to Charleston before the Indians were again on the warpath. They forced Fort Loudon to capitulate and as the garrison was making its way back they were surrounded by the Indians and all were killed or captured. General Amherst again came to the rescue by sending Colonel Grant, and another campaign was made against the Indians. Colonel Grant travelled over practically the same route that had been traversed by Montgomery. He also was surprised by the Indians at Echota but was successful in defeating them, after which Attakulkulla sued for peace.[38]

It was during this campaign that several prominent men of South Carolina saw action. They were Henry Laurens, John Moultrie, William Moultrie, Francis Marion, Isaac Huger, and Andrew Pickens.

The treaty of 1761 put to an end any further troubles with the Indians for a considerable length of time. Their next serious outbreak was to occur during the first years of the Revolutionary War.

Events were happening thick and fast in South Carolina during the later part of 1775. Lexington and Concord were events of the past. War with the mother country was certain. The part which South Carolina was to play was problematical, yet the patriots were striving for concerted action with the other colonies. However, there were many people in the upcountry, especially in the counties which were later to contribute to the settlement of Pendleton District, who were still loyal to the King. This was annoying to the Council of Safety, and its efforts for concerted Statewide action in the Revolution, together with the firm stand of these King's men, led to, what has been termed, an insurrection around Ninety Six.

The immediate cause was the arrest of Robert Cunningham on a charge of seditious words against the Government. So popular was Cunningham that many people rallied to his support.[40] Patrick Cunningham, with sixty followers, tried to rescue his brother who was being taken to the Charleston prison for confinement. They failed in the attempt, but knowing that the Council of Safety had sent ammunition to the Indians, which was to keep them on friendly terms with the Province, they determined to capture it. The capture was therefore made, and the reason given by Patrick Cunningham was that the ammunition was intended for the Indians who would use it against the King's men.[41] Upon hearing of the affair, the Council of Safety ordered Colonel Richardson to gather six companies for the purpose of suppressing the movement.[42] Colonel Bull and Lieutenant Mitchell, with men and field pieces, were also ordered to assist Richardson. This plainly showed the determination of the Council of Safety to suppress all disaffection in the colony.[43]

Captain Richard Pearis had now joined the disaffected group and made an affidavit that the powder which the Council of Safety had sent to the Indians was intended for use against the King's men. This statement strengthened the cause of the Loyalists.[44]

Major Williamson who had been encamped at Ninety Six was forced to withdraw before the approach of the Loyalist force. Slight skirmishes ensued between the two forces for a time when a treaty between them was signed. The agreement called for the disbanding of the armies and their differences submitted to the Governor and Council of Safety for settlement. In the meantime, Colonel Richardson had arrived at Ninety Six, and feeling that he was not bound by the agreement that had been made, proceeded to destroy the forces of the Loyalists.[45] This was easily accomplished because of the fact that many of the Loyalists had deserted, having lost confidence in their leaders. Richardson marched into the Indian lands where a remnant of the disaffected force was encamped, and completely dispersed it.[46] The suppression of this Loyalist movement around Ninety Six is called the Snow Campaign because of the fact that on December 23, 1775 it began snowing and continued for thirty hours, causing much suffering.[47]

The failure of the Loyalist movement was not the end of trouble for South Carolina. Richardson and others had hardly put it down before trouble started with the Indians. The danger from this Indian war was made worse by the fact that a number of white men and British agents were assisting them. The British Government with the assistance of these agents among the Indian tribes thus stirred up the Cherokees to a war in 1776. In this it was ably assisted by Captain John Stuart, Alexander Cameron, and Henry Stuart.[48]

It will be remembered that the Council of Safety, fearing such an uprising, in 1775 sent ammunition to the Indians, as a kind of peace offering. After the capture of this ammunition

Captain William Freeman was sent by the Government to meet the Indians and conciliate them. He reported that conciliation was impossible as long as Alexander Cameron lived among the Indians, for he had adopted their customs, and exerted a great influence over them. Therefore he thought that the capture of Cameron was necessary for the peace of the State.[49]

The Council of Safety ordered through Major Williamson, that Captain James McCall, associated with Captain James Baskin and Ensign Patrick Calhoun, should proceed to capture Cameron. They assembled at Cherokee Ford on the Savannah River with thirty three men, and marched into the Indian territory. They arranged a conference with the Indians, but while it was in session they were attacked. Most of the party managed to escape, but Patrick Calhoun was killed in the fight.[50]

The British agents persuaded the Cherokees to make an attack all along the frontiers from Georgia to Virginia at the same time that an English fleet and Army was to attack Charleston. On July 1, 1776, learning that the fleet and army were ready, the Indians swooped down upon the frontier with their usual cruelty. Many prominent settlers were killed, among them was the forebear of General Wade Hampton.[51]

Major Williamson, who had been promoted to the rank of Colonel, assembled four hundred and fifty men and encamped at Holmes' field on Hog Skin Creek. This point is about four miles from the Indian boundary and is now called Due West.[52] The people living on the Saluda River, in order to protect themselves better from the Indian attacks, moved into an old fort called Lyndley. On July 15 they were attacked by a number of Indians and white men. Fortunately for the fort, the evening before, Major Downes arrived with assistance and the attack failed.[53]

As soon as President Rutledge heard of the outbreak he sent a detachment of Rangers to the assistance of Williamson. In the meantime Williamson had heard of the failure of the British Fleet and Army against Charleston, and he renewed his preparations against the Indians. He had by this time assembled eleven hundred fifty men.[54]

Hearing that Cameron was encamped on Oconee Creek he planned to take him by surprise and put an end to his influence. With three hundred fifty men he entered the Cherokee Nation, and was soon opposite the Indian town of Essenneca on the banks of the Keowee River. There his force was surprised and attacked by the Indians and would have been completely repulsed had it not been for the efforts of Lieutenant Colonel Hammond who, by an impetuous charge with only about twenty men, restored order.[55]

The next day Williamson burnt Essenneca and proceeded further into the Indian territory. He destroyed many of the Indian towns in the lower settlements and completely defeated them in battle. After he had destroyed the lower settlements he was joined by General Rutherford of North Carolina, and together they finished the work of completely destroying the power of the Cherokees.[56]

On February 13, 1777, the General Assembly passed an Ordinance allowing the Governor to appoint five commissioners to treat for peace with the Indians who were then suing for peace.[57] A treaty was accordingly signed at De Witt's corner which gave all the Indian lands east of the Unacaye Mountains to South Carolina.[58] This treaty did not include quite all of what was finally given up, there being a small strip of land in the extreme northwestern part of the State which was not ceded until 1817. At this time the Indians relinquished all their territory which they once held in South Carolina.[59]

On page 11 is given a map showing the route taken by Colonel Williamson in this campaign. It included the principal Indian towns, the important streams, where he crossed them, and the places where fighting occured. It also contains a description of the Old Cherokee Path, used in former times by the Indians and early traders.

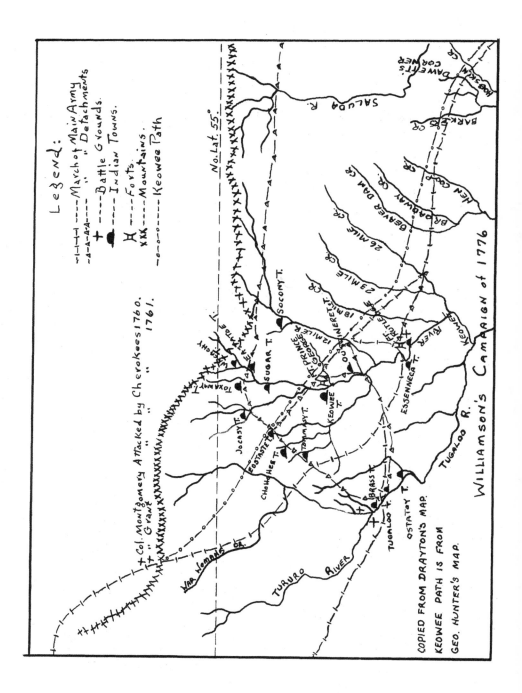

Legend:

⊢⊢⊢⊢ ---- March of Main Army
▲-▲-▲▲ ---- " " Detachments
✝ ---- Battle Grounds.
◖ ---- Indian Towns.
Ħ ---- Forts.
XXX ---- Mountains.
-o-o-o- ---- Keowee Path

✝ Col. Montgomery Attacked by Cherokees 1760.
✝ " Grant " " 1761.

No. Lat. 55°

SALUDA R.

DAWETT'S CORNER

HOGSKIN CR.

BARKERS CR.

NEW CR.

BROADAWAY CR.

BEAVER DAM CR.

26 MILE CR.

23 MILE CR.

18 MILE CR.

12 MILE CR.

Ft. PRINCE GEORGE

Ft. GEORGE

OCONEE T.

KEOWEE RIVER

ESSENNECA T.

TUGALOO R.

SOCONY T.

SUGAR T.

TOXAWAY T.

Jocasy

CHOTE

OSTATSTE T.

CHOW HEE T.

TOMMASY T.

KEOWEE T.

BRASS T.

OSTATOY T.

TUGALOO T.

WAR WOMANS CR.

TURURO RIVER

WILLIAMSON'S CAMPAIGN OF 1776.

COPIED FROM DRAYTON'S MAP.
KEOWEE PATH IS FROM
GEO. HUNTER'S MAP.

11

CHAPTER I FOOTNOTES

BIBLIOGRAPHY

1. Mills, Robert, <u>Statistics</u> <u>of</u> <u>South</u> <u>Carolina,</u> p. 673.

2. McLendon, W.E., <u>Soil</u> <u>Survey</u> <u>of</u> <u>Anderson</u> <u>County,</u> <u>South</u> <u>Carolina</u>, p. 6.

3. Watson, E.J., <u>Handbook</u> <u>of</u> <u>South</u> <u>Carolina,</u> p. 68.

4. McLendon, <u>op.</u> <u>cit.</u>, p. 6.

5. <u>Ibid.</u>, pp. 8-9.

6. <u>Ibid.</u>, p. 26.

7. <u>Ibid.</u>, p. 17.

8. McLendon, W.E., and Latimer, W.J., <u>Soil</u> <u>Survey</u> <u>of</u> <u>Oconee</u> <u>County,</u> <u>South</u> <u>Carolina</u>, p. 16.

9. No soil survey has been made of Pickens County, but studies have been made by A.H. Meyer of Clemson College, a letter from him concerning these soils is in the possession of the writer.

10. McClendon, W.E., <u>op.</u> <u>cit.</u>, p. 17.

11. <u>Ibid.</u>, p. 19.

12. <u>Ibid.</u>, p. .27.

13. Bartram, William, <u>The</u> <u>Travels,</u> pp. 380-81.

14. <u>Ibid.</u>, p. 381.

15. Crane, Verner C., <u>The</u> <u>Southern</u> <u>Frontier,</u> p. 41.

16. Bartram, <u>op.</u> <u>cit.</u>, p. 381.

17. <u>Ibid.</u>, pp. 296-97.

18. <u>Ibid.</u>, pp. 297-98.

19. Drayton, J., <u>Memoirs</u> <u>of</u> <u>the</u> <u>American</u> <u>Revolution,</u> vol. I, p. 428.

20. Crane, <u>op.</u> <u>cit.</u>, p. 115

21. <u>Ibid.</u>, p. 22.

22. <u>Council</u> <u>Journals,</u> vol. 18, pp. 509-11.

23. McCrady, E., <u>The</u> <u>History</u> <u>of</u> <u>South</u> <u>Carolina</u> <u>under</u> <u>the</u> <u>Royal</u> <u>Government,</u> pp. 270-71.

24. Was living in Pendleton District in 1790.

25. Logan, J.H., <u>A</u> <u>History</u> <u>of</u> <u>the</u> <u>Upper</u> <u>Country</u> <u>of</u> <u>South</u> <u>Carolina,</u> vol. I, p. 434.

26. Crane, <u>op. cit.</u>, p. 125.

27. Council Journals, <u>op. cit.</u>, p. 513.

28. Crane, <u>op. cit.</u>, pp. 124-25.

29. George Hunter's Map of 1730.

30. Crane, <u>op. cit.</u>, p. 129.

31. Ramsay, David, <u>History of South Carolina,</u> vol. I, p. 166.

32. <u>Ibid.</u>, pp. 167-68.

33. Ramsay, <u>op. cit.</u>, pp. 170-73.

34. <u>Ibid.</u>, pp. 174-75.

35. McCrady, <u>op. cit.</u>, p. 331.

36. Ramsay, <u>op. cit.</u>, pp. 176-80.

37. <u>Ibid.</u>, p. 190.

38. Ramsay, <u>op. cit.</u>, p. 197.

39. <u>Ibid.</u>, p. 185.

40. Drayton, <u>op. cit.</u>, pp. 60-61.

41. <u>Ibid.</u>

42. <u>Ibid.</u>, pp. 64-68.

43. <u>Ibid.</u>, pp. 81-82.

44. <u>Ibid.</u>, pp. 117-19.

45. <u>Ibid.</u>, pp. 120-28.

46. <u>Ibid.</u>, pp. 128-32.

47. <u>Ibid.</u>, pp. 132-37.

48. Drayton, <u>op. cit.</u>, vol. 2, pp. 338-39.

49. McCrady, <u>op. cit.</u>, vol. 3, pp. 187-89.

50. <u>Ibid.</u>

51. Ramsay, <u>op. cit.</u>, p. 339.

52. <u>Ibid.</u>, p. 341.

53. <u>Ibid.</u>, pp. 342-44.

54. <u>Ibid.</u>, p. 344.

55. Ibid., pp. 345-46.

56. Ibid., pp. 351-52.

57. Statutes At Large of South Carolina, vol. IV, pp. 391-92.

58. Ramsay, op. cit., p. 124.

59. Logan, op. cit., vol. I, pp. 504-05.

II. SETTLEMENT OF PENDLETON DISTRICT.

In 1755 Braddock was defeated and the frontiers of Pennsylvania, Virginia, and Maryland were exposed to danger from Indian attacks. As a result, many people from this section migrated southward, and some of the immigrants reached the lower edge of what later became Pendleton District. [1] A considerable number of Scotch-Irish from Pennsylvania were in this southward movement. They followed the foot of the mountains, spreading from Staunton, Virginia to the Waxhaws. From this point they proved a great factor in settling the upcountry. [2] Settlement went forward rather rapidly in the upper part of the colony until 1759, when several settlements were broken up by the Indians, and the movement was checked for a time. However, the Peace of Paris in 1763 removed much of the danger from the Indians, and the process of settlement again received an impetus. [3]

The territory, which later became Pendleton District, was still in the possession of the Indians. A desire for gain, adventure, and new homes, pushed the frontiersmen closer to this section, and this disturbed the Indians. As Bartram analyzed the Cherokees, one of their chief characteristics was a tenacious desire for their rights against the encroachment of their territory. Consequently, from the Cherokee War to the outbreak of the Revolution, settlement near the Indian territory was slow. There were a few however, who settled near the boundary line, and undoubtedly, some who crossed into the Indian territory. In 1765 the Governor received a message from the Cherokees, asking that a line be run between them and the English to prevent disputes. Due to the fertility of the land, settlers were gradually drawn to the land of the Indians. [4]

Again in 1765 trouble was brewing. Benjamin Brown, Edward Box, and Richard Owens, referred to by Ensign Price of Fort Prince George as "Crackers", were living on Raeburn's Creek. They were captured by the Indians and taken to Fort Prince George for confinement. The Indians charged horse theft, and in turn, the whites charged outrages. Both sides petitioned the Governor for redress, but the Attorney General held that the colony lacked jurisdiction. He suggested that the prisoners be released, but if they continued in their mischief, they should be placed under bond, and if they failed in giving surety, committed to prison. [5]

This trouble and the Indian request brought action. The Governor gave orders that a line be run between the Indians and the settlers. The line was to extend so as to include the outermost surveys of land, but after the establishment of such a line, no further grants would be made beyond it.[6] The line suggested by Mr. Pickens, who had been appointed surveyor, leaves no doubt concerning the encroachment of the settlers to and into the Indian territory. He suggested that the line begin near Brodie's plantation and continue to the Tugaloo Path where it would turn in a southwesterly course until it intersected the Savannah River. In commenting on this line, the Governor said that it would include those settlers on Ross' Creek and Campbell's plantation. The line on the north side of Brodie's plantation was to keep the creek to its head, and from thence in a northeasterly direction till it intersected the Saluda or Reedy River. This line would take in all remote settlers except a few. Patrick Calhoun had informed the Governor that several thousand acres of land had been run out east of the Beaver Dams, but provision was to be made with the Indians for the security of these settlers.[7] This indicates that settlers were near the Cherokee lands and a few actually within it.

Another indication of settlement near and possibly within the Cherokee territory is found in a statement made by Rev. William Tennant. On his tour through the upper country in 1775, which was made to enlighten the people of that section of the State concerning the true condition of affairs between Great Britain and the Colonies, he visited many places, one of which was Bull Town, in Abbeville, fifteen miles from the Indian line. He spoke to the People at the meeting-house, and "to one of the most crowded assemblies he ever saw."[8] This would indicate that many people were living in this section, or else his "crowded assembly" traveled from miles around, some probably coming from the Indian lands.

The tendency to settle in and near the Pendleton District received a check between 1770 and 1776. During this period the British agents were busy among the Indians and secured their assistance in the Revolutionary War. However, in 1777 they were defeated and ceded their lands to the state of South Carolina, which threw open for settlement all of their lands east of the Unacaye Mountains,[9] or at least made it possible for settlement to begin as soon as a law was passed providing for such

16

settlement.

The act of granting this land was not begun until 1784. However, exceptions are found. In 1773, even before the acquisition of the territory, the state made a grant of land to William Lawrence on Cherokee Creek of Rocky River in what is now Anderson County.[10]

Bartram in his Travels, records the fact that there were a few inhabitants in this section. In making a trip from Dartmouth to Fort Prince George during the month of May, 1775, he called the country "an uninhabited wilderness." The section which was traversed by him were the present counties of Anderson and Pickens. Leaving Dartmouth on the Savannah River, he came to Mr. Cameron's , a deputy commissioner to the Indians, whose residence was about forty-five miles north of Dartmouth. This would place Cameron in the lower edge of Pendleton District or the upper part of Abbeville.[11] From here he proceeded to Fort Prince George on the east bank of Keowee River in the present county of Pickens. Here he found Mr. D. Holmes the principal trader residing at the old fort. He stated that there were no Indian inhabitants but several dwellings were occupied by white people who were chiefly concerned in the Indian trade.[12]

After the acquisition of the Cherokee territory in 1777, no law was passed for granting these lands until 1784. This delay was undoubtedly due to the Revolution. During the period, 1777 to 1784, some people went into this territory, but the number can not be definitely ascertained. In 1778 an Act was passed dealing with this question. At the time, the newly acquired Indian lands had not been placed within the bounds of any judicial circuit, and no Justices of the Peace had jurisdiction over it. Consequently, many vagrants, without any authority, went upon these lands, with the intention of eluding certain laws of the State. Particularly, those by which troops were being raised for the Continental Service. As a result of the evasion of this law, the lately ceded Indian lands were placed in Ninety-Six District, thus giving the officials of Ninety-Six jurisdiction.[13] As the Act indicates, people had no legal right to settle in the new area, yet they did and helped to swell the number who subsequently made it their home.

As previously stated, in 1784 a law was passed providing a

system of granting land in the area which later became Pendleton District. The reason for the passage of this law was evidently due to the number of people already settled there, and to others desirous of making it their home.

The people who had gone into these new lands might be termed "Squatters". They had located on land but as yet did not have a title for it. Some of these might have been only temporary settlers such as the vagrants who tried to evade Continental Service; but there were others who settled there with the idea of making it their permanent home. This is evidenced by a law passed in 1784 dealing with just such a class. It stated that, those before January 1, 1775, who had located lands on warrants of survey, legally obtained, and had been prevented from procuring grants for the lands occupied, either by the British Government or any other good and sufficient cause, could obtain grants if they would make application to the commissioner of location in their district within a period of six months after the passage of the Act.[14] This Act was especially applicable to that portion of the State just recently acquired from the Indians.[15] It is therefore natural to suppose that settlers were there, not only between 1777 and 1784, but even before January 1, 1775.

In this same Act, the exact method of granting land was outlined. It provided for a commissioner of location for each circuit court with two for Ninety-Six District. One of these commissioners was to reside north and the other south of the Saluda River. Their duties were to take and receive the original entries of all vacant lands, and to direct a deputy surveyor to lay off and locate lands to be surveyed. When a warrant for land was received with a true and correct plat of survey, the commissioner was to make a fair record of it and within three months transmit it to the office of the Surveyor General.[16] From this the Surveyor General was to make out a plat of the land surveyed, record it and transmit it to the Secretary of State, who in turn was to prepare the grant. After recording it, the grant was ready for the signature of the Governor and the Great Seal of the State.[17]

The price of land was fixed at ten pounds sterling for each one hundred acres.[18] However, in 1785, this was changed to ten dollars for one hundred acres. Warrants of survey not paid for within three months were to become null and void, and could be

18

resold to another person. No warrant was to exceed 640 acres, and the land had to be cultivated twelve months before it could be sold. Specific instructions were given that no surveys should be made beyond the Indian boundary, the violation of which would automatically make the survey null and of no force.[19]

The rush of people into this territory called attention to political reforms that appeared necessary. Therefore, on March 16, 1783, the General Assembly appointed commissioners to divide the State into counties.[20] These new divisions were not to exceed forty square miles in area unless the growing population or the situation of the land required a deviation.[21] The commissioners appointed for the division of the Ninety-Six District were Andrew Pickens, Richard Anderson, Thomas Brandon, Levi Keysey, Philemon Waters, Arthur Simkins, and Simon Berwick.[22] One of the duties imposed upon them was that of recommending a proper place for the county seat of government. The location was to be selected as near the center of the county as possible. The court house, jails, and other public buildings necessary for county government were to be located at the county seat.[23]

Several counties were formed out the the Ninety-Six District. Those in the upper part of the district were Greenville and Pendleton. The boundaries of Greenville County[24] are described as "Saluda River and the south fork thereof, the old Indian boundary, and the North Carolina line."[25] Pendleton County had the following boundaries: "beginning at Savannah River and running along the old Indian boundary line, which divided it from Abbeville County, to Saluda River; thence up the said river to the new Indian boundary; thence along the said boundary line to the Toogaloo river; thence down the said river and Savannah river to the Beginning." The above was accomplished March 7, 1789.[26]

The judicial division of this part of the State remained unchanged until January 19, 1791. At this time a new district was created and the name of Washington was given to it. The counties of Greenville and Pendleton made up the Washington District, and its courts were to have jurisdiction in all civil and criminal cases.[27] By an Act of 1792, Pickensville, about one mile south of the present town of Easley, was named as the district seat of government. Pickensville was built on lands conveyed to the Commissioners by Charles Cotesworth Pinckney. The new district was named Washington, probably due to the fact that the President made a visit to South Carolina in 1791, stopping in Columbia on May 22, 23, and 24.[29]

Washington District did not enjoy a long existence. On December 21, 1798, it was divided, and the western portion became Pendleton District. Its bounds were "to comprehend the county of that name, according to its present limits."[30] This continual cutting of the territory into smaller judicial divisions was made necessary by the rapid increase of population.

Pendleton County as well as District was named in compliment to Henry Pendleton. He was a native of Virginia and after immigrating to South Carolina became a prominent and distinguished citizen. He acted in the capacity of judge for the court of Common Pleas as well as serving in the Legislature on several occasions.[31]

The county seat of Pendleton District was the village of Pendleton. It consisted of a court house, jail, a Presbyterian Church, an Episcopal Church, forty houses, an Academy, a printing office issuing a weekly paper, and an agricultural hall.[32]

Pendleton District remained in existence until 1828 when it was divided into Pickens and Anderson Districts.[33] Pickens and Anderson counties were formed in 1826, but in 1828 the Act was passed making them judicial districts.[34]

It is evident that quite a number of people located lands and made application for a grant, yet they never received a title, due to the fact that they could not or would not pay. To meet the situation the Assembly on various occasions extended the time for making payment.[35] Thus years sometimes passed between the time of survey and the actual granting of the land. As an illustration of this, a careful survey has been made of the state Record of Plats, and during the period from 1777 to 1800, only 599 grants and plats are to be found. This represents about ninety five per cent of the total number of grants made. These same records show that there were 735 squatters, occupying lands adjacent to the actual land holders.[36] These with many more, as shown by the United States Census of 1790, had no grants for these lands, and it is but natural to infer that this law was passed for the benefit of such people. The records in the office of the Secretary of State show that practically all of these people secured their grants after 1800. This policy of extending the time of payment evidently slowed up the securing of grants and made it appear that few settlers were in the district.

The exact number of people living in Pendleton District prior to 1800 can not be definitely known. From the Plat and Grant records in the office of the Secretary of State it would appear that the number was small. However, the United States Census of 1790 and 1800 give another impression. The difference is that the State Records show the actual number holding lands, while the Census gives all persons residing within the district. The Census of 1790 for South Carolina shows that there were living within the bounds of what later became Pendleton District 9,568 people, which included the following classifications: Number of Heads of Families, 1,433; Free White Males of Sixteen Years and Upwards, 2,007; Free White Males under Sixteen, 2,535; Free White Females including Heads of Families, 4,189; All Other Free Persons, 3; Slaves, 834.[37] The Census of 1800 shows that the population exceeded twenty thousand. Of this number 17,670 were whites, and 2,224 were slaves, and 68 were free blacks.[38]

Following is a list of those people living in the district in 1790, according to the United States Census of 1790, and the names of those according to the State Record of Land Grants who were living there as squatters, together with the year in which they came into possession of their land. If they had just settled in the district in 1790, it required from one to nine years for them to secure their grants, and it is entirely probable that they were there before 1790, thus making the period of time in which they are termed squatters, much longer.

Abbet, James	1793	Fitzgerrel, Ambose	1799
Anderson, William.	1791	Fuller, Mordica	1795
Armstrong, John.	1791	Garner, Thomas	1792
Austen, Nathen	1791	Graham, Edward	1792
Beesley, William	1796	Grant, William	1801
Brown, Elijah	1792	Gray, William	1797
Burch, Henry	1799	Green, Henry	1791
Burney, William	1792	Hamilton, John	1798
Burns, Alexander	1793	Hamilton, William	1798
Butt, John	1799	Harden, John	1793
Capehart, Jacob.	1795	Haney, Charles	1797
Clark, Micajah	1799	Harper, John	1799
Crawford, James	1795	Haynie, John	1795
Davis, Eli	1798	Harkins, Hugh	1797
Dobson, Henry	1798	Holland, Jacob	1799
Dromgoole, Alexander	1791	Honey, William	1799
Duncan, Joseph	1797	Hickman, Benjamin	1794
Edens, Alexander	1798	Hood, John	1797
Farrar, Leonard.	1794	Hutson, George	1798

Irby, Isham 1796			Simpson, Reuben 1792	
Jones, Moses 1798			Sloan, David 1791	
Prator, Philip 1791			Whorton, Benjamin . . . 1792	

The Appendix contains a table giving the entire population of the district in 1790. This list was taken from the United States Census for South Carolina.

The problem of ascertaining the origin of the settlers of Pendleton District is a difficult one. However, it appears that there were two main sources of immigration. One of these was removals within the State from the south toward the north. The other was an influx from Pennsylvania, Maryland, Virginia, North Carolina, and Georgia.[39] As proof of the above, in 1790, the following people were found living in various parts of South Carolina, as indicated in the table. They later removed to Pendleton District.[40]

Adair, John	Laurens County
Arnold, Benjamin	Greenville County
Bacon, Thomas	Edgefield County
Bell, William	Orangeburg County
Boyd, Thomas	Orangeburg County
Bradley, James	Greenville County
Brown, Jesse	Cheraw County
Burton, Josiah	Abbeville County
Caldwell, John	Newberry County
Calvert, John	Edgefield County
Chapman, Samuel	Newberry County
Cobb, Humphry	Greenville County
Courtney, James	Cheraw County
Craig, John	Laurens County
Curry, James	Laurens County
Dickey, James	Clarendon County
England, Charles	Laurens County
Edwards, John	Spartanburg County
Entrekin, John	Laurens County
Eubanks, John	Union County
George, Britain	Spartanburg County
Gilder, Isaac	Newberry County
Gillaspie, James	Abbeville County
Green, Elisha	Edgefield County
Grissum, John	Fairfield County
Hays, John	Cheraw County
Hickman, William	Spartanburg County
Hillhouse, John	York County
Howard, Abraham	Abbeville County
Hudson, John, Sr.	Beaufort District
Kilpatrick, William	Newberry County
Philips, Jacob.	Abbeville County
Plunkett, Charley	Newberry County
Richards, William	Newberry County
Rutherford, James	Edgefield County

This list accounts for thirty-five land holders of Pendleton District, all coming from South Carolina, and in the majority of cases from the upper part of the State

The same records show that seventeen of the land holders of the district come from North Carolina, and are as follows:

Bobbitt, William . . . . . . Hillsborough District-Chatham Co.
Bynum, John . . . . Hillsborough District-Orange Co.
Boyse, Robert . . . . Edenton District-Bertie Co.
Clements, James . . . . . . Morgan District-Burke Co.
Carpenter, Thomas . . . . . Halifax District-Nash Co.
Darnall, William . . . . . . Salisbury District-Mecklenbury Co.
Dickson, Samuel H. . . . . . Hillsborough District-Chatham Co.
Durley, Arthur . . . . Halifax District-Nash Co.
Durram, William . . . . . . Morgan District-Rutherford Co.
Ellis, James . . . . Hillsborough District-Chatham Co.
Fariss, William . . . . . . Morgan District-Rutherford Co.
Fields, Jerimiah . . . . . . Salisbury District-Guilford Co.
Glenn, William . . . . Salisbury District-Rockingham Co.
Guy, William . . . . Wilmington District-Duplin Co.
Kennedy, William Ebenezer. . Fayette District-Cumberland Co.
Kilpatrick, James . . . . . Morgan District-Rutherford Co.
Ledbetter, Joel . . . . . . Hillsborough District-Caswell Co.

The Virginia contribution to the settlement of Pendleton District was not as large as some of the rest, yet there came from this State eight which are given below:

Bole, James . . . . Chesterfield County
Boulgar, Michael . . . . . . Hampshire County
Brown, Benjamin, Capt. . . . Cumberland County
Burton, Samuel . . . . Princess Anne County
Clark, Micajah . . . . Albemarle County
Drummond, James . . . . . . City of Richmond
Eckols, Joshua . . . . Pittsylvania County
Hendricks, Moses . . . . . . Halifax County

Pendleton District was also supplied with fifteen settlers from the State of Maryland which are as follows:

Brown, Benjamin . . . . . . Baltimore County
Bush, William . . . . Queens Ann County
Clark, Micajah . . . . Frederick County
Clements, Charles . . . . . Charles County
Combs, Bennett . . . . St. Marys County
Corrie, John . . . . Talbot County
Davis, Alexander . . . . . . Worcester County
Evans, Ezekiel . . . . Frederick County
Glenn, William . . . . Kent County
Green, Abednigo. . . . . . . Baltimore County
Herrin, Elijah . . . . Frederick County
Hutton, Joseph . . . . Frederick County
Kilgore, James . . . . Cecil County
Lamar, Thomas. . . . . Frederick County
Naylor, George . . . . Prince George County

The Census tables show that there were nine people living in Pennsylvania in 1790 who subsequently removed to Pendleton District. They were:

```
Barton, Stephens . . . . . . . Bucks County
Beard, Thomas   . . . . . . . . Northampton County
Calhoun, John. . . . . . . . . Franklin County
Dickson, Samuel. . . . . . . . Westmoreland County
Dougherty, Joseph. . . . . . . Lancaster County
Dyer, Joshua . . . . . . . . . Bucks County
Faust, Jacob . . . . . . . . . Berks County
Fullerton, Robert. . . . . . . York County
Huston, James. . . . . . . . . Cumberland County
```

Although immigration at this period was flowing westward, yet there were few people from the State of Georgia that stemmed the tide, coming eastward into the Pendleton District. This was a bit unusual, but the causes probably justified their action. In 1782, the Georgia Assembly passed an Act of Attainder, banishing from the State and confiscating their property, many citizens who had been disloyal to the cause of the Revolution. Sixty days were given them to make their departure or to suffer imprisonment. Checking this list of disloyal people with the United States Census of 1790 for South Carolina, and also with the State Record of Land Grants, the following were found to be living in Pendleton District.[41]

GEORGIA LOYALISTS	RECEIVED GRANTS	STREAMS SQUATTED UPON
Brown, James		Cain
Brown, Thomas	1789	
Brown, William	1784	
Clark, William	1787	
Glen, John		
Graham, James	1785	
Johnson, John	1785	
Manson, William		
Maxwell, John		Hen Coop Creek
Miller, Robert		
McLain, Alexander		
Thomas, John		
Thompson, James		Beaver Creek
Young, John		Hen Coop Creek
Young, William		Little Eastatoe Creek

The above tables represent 16.6 percent of the settlers in Pendleton District who had been granted land between 1777 and 1800. While this is not a large percent, yet it gives a fair impression as to the origin of settlers making Pendleton District their home.

The question now arises as to the actual place of settlement of those people within the district. The logical arrangement of such settlement is to group the time from 1777 to 1800 into periods.

The first period will fall between the dates of 1777 to 1791 when the territory was included within the bounds of Ninety-Six District; the second between 1791 and 1798 when it was called Washington District; the third will include the remaining time from 1798 to 1800 when the territory was actually Pendleton District. (The Pendleton District, however, lasted until 1828.) With this grouping in mind, the accompanying maps are used to show the distribution of the people over the district and their actual place of settlement. These maps show not only the streams upon which settlement was made, but also the number locating upon each stream. The exact number of people settling according to the above periods is given. They indicate the approximate number of acres of land granted and where the grant was made. The numbers corresponding to each square refer to the Table of Settlement to be found in the Appendix with the exact information concerning each settler.

It is practically impossible to locate accurately each land holder. However, in many cases a large degree of correctness is entirely possible. People settling in the forks of streams are easy to locate. Those taking up land on roads and Indian paths cause no trouble. Furthermore, many settlers of prominence, who were living on lines surveyed by the State, as boundary lines, are generally placed on old maps of the district. Some plats give very accurately the exact place of location. With the aid of such material, practically all grants approach a close degree of accuracy. None of the grants of land on the accompanying maps could be out of place more than one mile.

SUMMARY

The Pendleton District, composed of the present counties of Anderson, Oconee, and Pickens, was secured from the Cherokees by the treaty of 1777. The county of Greenville was also a part of this acquisition, but due to its own geographical unity, being distinct and separate from that of the Pendleton area, it is not treated in this work.

Pendleton District was primarily agricultural. Its principal soils, the Cecil sandy loam and Meadow, were well adapted to farming, and produced a fair crop the first year of cultivation. This was a big factor in encouraging settlers to make this territory their home. The principal crop was corn, yet its soils and climate conditions were most favorable for fruit growing.

The Cherokee Indians occupied this territory prior to 1777, and were the most civilized of all the southern Indian tribes. Their wars with the whites were similar to most Indian wars, accompanied with outrages of various kinds, and this menace kept back settlement for quite a while.

The Loyalist movement around Ninety-Six, during the early days of the Revolution had, to some extent, a bearing upon the settlement of Pendleton District. First of all, it was near the Pendleton District, and on several occasions, fighting occurred within its limits. This no doubt gave a better knowledge of the soil to the soldiers of both sides, causing many of them to settle there.

The early Indian trader was the forerunner of settlement. He lived with the Indians, acquired a thorough knowledge of the country, and with his trade and traffic was a great assistance to the settlement of the district. It was his knowledge of conditions in the Indian country, combined with the hardihood of the settlers themselves, that ultimately overcame both the Indian and nature.

Settlement began very early in Pendleton District. People were locating there by 1775, before it was acquired by the State. This was one cause of disturbances with the Indians. In 1784 the State provided with proper legislation for the permanent settlement of the district. Those in the district prior to that time are termed squatters, and even after that date, many failed to secure a title to the lands they had located upon. Laws were passed at various times to help this class of people, by extending the time for payment of land, and many of them with this assistance failed to secure their grants until after 1800.

Settlers to Pendleton District came from many parts of the United States, Pennsylvania, Maryland, Virginia, North Carolina, South Carolina, and Georgia contributed to the settlement. They scattered over the district, locating on streams, as shown by the maps of settlement. The channels of immigration into this territory was from the south to the north, as far as South Carolina was concerned, yet there was a settlement movement for those people who came from the northern colonies. They came

26

principally by way of the Waxhaw settlement, spreading over the district in various directions.

With the acquisition of this territory in 1777, South Carolina was rounded out to its present shape and size. At the time it was practically an uninhabited wilderness, yet it consisted of approximately 2,000,000 acres of land. This territory went through many political changes. It was first embraced in the Ninety Six District. In 1791 it became Washington District, and in 1796 was changed to the Pendleton District. It remained thus until 1828. Today, what was once called the Pendleton District is known as Anderson, Oconee, and Pickens counties.

CHAPTER II FOOTNOTES

BIBLIOGRAPHY

1.   Mills, Robert, op. cit., p. 672.

2.   McCrady, op. cit., p. 312.

3.   Mills, op. cit., p. 672.

4.   Journals of the House of Representatives, vol. 37, p. 3.

5.   Council Journals, vol. 32, pp. 558-61.

6.   Ibid.

7.   Ibid.

8.   Howe, George, History of the Presbyterian Church in South
       Carolina, p. 363.

9.   Mills, op. cit., p. 672.

10. State Record of Land Plats, vol. 16, p. 290.

11. Bartram, William, The Travels, pp. 266-69.

12. Ibid., p. 271.

13. Cooper, Thomas, Statues At Large of South Carolina, vol.
       Fourth, p. 411.

14. Ibid., p. 590.

15. Ibid.

16. Ibid.

17. Ibid., pp. 591-92.

18. Ibid., p. 590.

19. Ibid., pp. 592-93.

20. Ibid., p. 561.

21. Ibid.

22. Ibid.

23. Ibid.

24. Greenville County was a part of the territory acquired from
       the Indians in 1777, yet it is set off by natural
       boundaries from Pendleton District and is a unit to
       itself. Therefore, no attempt has been made to treat of
       its settlement.

25. Ibid., vol. 7, p. 245.

26. _Ibid._, pp. 252-53.

27. _Ibid._, p. 262.

28. _Ibid._, vol. V, p. 210.

29. Chapman, J.A., _School History of South Carolina,_ pp. 157-58.

30. _Statutes At Large of South Carolina,_ vol. VII, p. 284.

31. Ramsay, _op. cit._, p. 295.

32. Mills, _op cit._, p. 674.

33. _Statutes At Large of South Carolina,_ vol. VI, p. 341.

34. _Ibid._

35. _Ibid._, p. 747 and also _Ibid._, vol. Fifth, p. 207.

36. Reference made to Table of Settlement in Appendix which was compiled from _State Record of Land Plats_ in office of the Secretary of State, Columbia, S.C.

37. _Heads of Families of South Carolina,_ 1790, U.S. Census.

38. United States Census Report of 1800.
    Mills, _op. cit._, p. 678.

39. Howe, _op. cit._, p. 643.

40. Record of Land Plats were checked with the United States Census of 1790 for the States of South Carolina, North Carolina, Virginia, Maryland, and Pennsylvania.

41. _The Revolutionary Records of the State of Georgia,_ vol.1, p. 373-97.

III. APPENDIX

A. Bounty Land Holders.

The General Assembly passed an Act in 1778 reserving certain lands for the soldiers of South Carolina who served in the Revolutionary War. The territory between the Keowee and Tugaloo rivers was set aside for this purpose. No grants in this section were legal until after the war and all soldiers had received their portions. Each soldier was to be granted two hundred acres including the one hundred acres allowed by Congress, and the transfer was to be made free of expense to him. The grant was a title in fee simple and was a reward for his services.

The following is a list of the soldiers who took advantage of this law and received the bounty between 1777 and 1800:

Name	Acres	Name	Acres
Baker, Jesse Capt.	300	Blair,Wade	200
Bottle, Robert	200	Bowling, James	200
Bowie, John, Capt.	300	Bowie, John	200
Brough, George	200	Brough, James	200
Bush, John, Lt., Heirs	200	Chambers, Peter	200
Chavees, John	200	Clappard, John	200
Clark, Gideon	200	Crowley, Charles, Capt.	450
Currell, John	200	Davis, Harmin	300
Denton, Reuben	200	Driggs, Devereaux	200
Donnam, William	300	Doyley, James, Lt.	200
Dunbar, Thomas	200	Eason, John	200
Edmunds, David	200	Ellient, Andrew D. Maj.	400
Elliott, Hanard	300	Ernest, John	300
Feast, James	200	Gadsden, Thomas, Capt.	300
Gamball, James	200	Giles, Thomas	400
Gillen, Alexander, Esq.	400	Goodwyn, Uriah	300
Grimke, John F., Lt.	450	Grooms, Gilbert	200
Hamilton, James, Jr.	200	Harlston, Isaac, Maj.	400
Hext, William, Capt.	300	Holland, John	200
Huggins, John	200	Leonard, Lachlin	200
Lidle, George, Capt.	300	Merick, William	200
Milligan, Jacob	450	Mills, Gilbert	200
Moore, Thomas	200	Murphey, Edward	200
McGee, John	200	Nevin, James	200
Nixon, Alexander	200	Norris, Daniel	200
Parsons, William	300	Pollard, Richard	300
Riddle, William	200	Roberts, Richard	300
Robertson, James	200	Russell, Thomas Com.	200
St. Marie, Levacher de,		Scarff, Joseph	200
Capt.	300	Scott, James	200
Scott, William, Lt. Col.	450	Shubrick, Thomas, Capt.	300
Skelton, John	200	Smith, Aaron	200
Spence, John	200	Spence, Robert	110
Sunn, Frederick, Dr.	300	Turner, Eleaser	200
Waddle, James	200	Walker, Joseph	200
Weaver, Thomas, Capt.	300	White, Thomas, Lt.	300
Wise, Samuel, Maj.	400	Wood, Benjamin	200

TABLE OF SETTLEMENT

B. TABLE OF SETTLEMENT, 1777-1800

No.	Stream	Name	Acre	Date	Bounded By	Reference
1	Cain Cr.	James Jett	202	1799		v. 37, p. 239
2	Cain Cr.	John Attenson	200	1784		v. 15q, p. 79
3	Cain Cr.	George Ashford	163	1789		v. 24q, p. 295
4	Cain Cr.				John Brown	v. 24q, p. 295
5	Cain Cr.				John White	v. 24q, p. 295
6	Cain Cr.				Wm. Betheney	v. 24q, p. 295
7	Cain Cr.				Isaac Hollingsworth	v. 24q, p. 295
8	Cain Cr.	Gideon Clark	200	1784		v. 13q, p. 195
9	Cain Cr.	Humphry Cobb	736	1792		v. 28q, p. 347
10	Cain Cr.				Faila Paucet	v. 28q, p. 347
11	Cain Cr.	Wade Blair	200	1784		v. 15q, p. 61
12	Cain Cr.				John Muloster	v. 15q, p. 61
13	Cain Cr.	John Bowers	100	1784		v. 3q, p. 41
14	Cain Cr.				Benj. Hawkins	v. 3q, p. 41
15	Cain Cr.	Wm. Sloan	310	1791		v. 27q, p. 411
16	Cain Cr.	West Gorly	415	1798		v. 36, p. 175
17	Cain Cr.				----- Beesley	v. 36, p. 175
18	Cain Cr.				Wm. Thompson	v. 36, p. 175
19	Conneros Cr.	John Butt	57½	1799		v. 37, p. 443
20	Conneros Cr.	Michael Byrd	171	1798		v. 37, p. 91
21	Conneros Cr.	Wm. Kilpatrick	270	1798		v. 37, p. 98
22	Conneros Cr.	Major Parsons	466	1798		v. 37, p. 98

Table of Settlement, cont'd.

No.	Location	Name	Acres	Year	Reference
23	Conneros Cr.	Thomas Lamar	300	1798	v. 36, p. 174
24	Conneros Cr.	----- Sheinger			v. 36, p. 174
25	Conneros Cr.	----- Robberd			v. 36, p. 174
26	Conneros Cr.	----- Kanin			v. 36, p. 174
27	Conneros Cr.	Wm. Kilpatrick	270	1798	v. 37, p. 98
28	Conneros Cr.	James Anderson			v. 37, p. 98
29	Conneros Cr.	Robert Anderson			v. 37, p. 98
30	Conneros Cr.	John Williams			v. 37, p. 98
31	Conneros Cr.	Jas. Kilpatrick			v. 37, p. 98
32	Conneros Cr.	Wm. Little			v. 37, p. 98
33	Conneros Cr.	Robert Speed			v. 37, p. 98
34	Conneros Cr.	Jas. Kilpatrick	400	1797	v. 36, p. 58
35	Conneros Cr.	Alex. Kilpatrick			v. 36, p. 58
36	Conneros Cr.	John Williams			v. 36, p. 58
37	Conneros Cr.	Wm. Little			v. 36, p. 58
38	Conneros Cr.	Solomon Perkins			v. 36, p. 58
39	Conneros Cr.	Wm. Twitty			v. 36, p. 58
40	Conneros Cr.	James Brough	200	1784	v. 13q, p. 236
41	Conneros Cr.	John Davey			v. 13q, p. 236
42	Conneros Cr.	Nathen Austin	150	1791	v. 25q, p. 370
43	Conneros Cr.	Robt. Buchannan	200	1784	v. 15q, p. 70
44	Conneros Cr.	Daniel Campbell	296	1789	v. 24q, p. 54
45	Conneros Cr.	John Bowie	200	1785	v. 13q, p. 237
46	Conneros Cr.	Capt. Jno. Bowie	300	1784	v. 13q, p. 243
47	Conneros Cr.	Hugh Kirkland			v. 13q, p. 243

No.	Stream	Name	Acre	Date	Bounded By	Reference
48	Conneros Cr.				Chas. Nicholas	v. 13q, p. 243
49	Conneros Cr.	Geo. Brough	200	1784		v. 13q, p. 238
50	Conneros Cr.				Capt. Uriah Goodwyn	v. 13q, p. 238
51	Conneros Cr.	Wm. Gray	300	1785		v. 11q, p. 320
52	Conneros Cr.				Francis Miller	v. 11q, p. 320
53	Conneros Cr.	Peter Gray	300	1784		v. 13q, p. 211
54	Conneros Cr.	Dr. Peter Fayssaux	500	1784		v. 11q, p. 105
55	Conneros Cr.	Capt. Chas. Crowley	450	1784		v. 13q, p. 201
56	Conneros Cr.	Barnard Elliott	300	1784		v. 13q, p. 207
57	Conneros Cr.	Uriah Goodwyn	300	1784		v. 13q, p. 241
58	Conneros Cr.	Adj. & Lieut. Jno. Hamilton	300	1784		v. 13q, p. 229
59	Conneros Cr.	Jno. Harrison	200	1784		v. 13q, p. 233
60	Conneros Cr.				Robert Buchannan	v. 13q, p. 233
61	Conneros Cr.	Jno. Lawrence	200	1785		v. 7q, p. 120
62	Conneros Cr.				Robert Waddel	v. 7q, p. 120
63	Conneros Cr.	Charles Lay	1000	1787		v. 19q, p. 233
64	Conneros Cr.	Alex. Nixon	200	1784		v. 12q, p. 182
65	Conneros Cr.	Dennes O'Brian	200	1784		v. 12q, p. 348
66	Conneros Cr.				Stephen Mazyck	v. 12q, p. 348
67	Conneros Cr.				Jno. Grayson	v. 12q, p. 348
68	Conneros Cr.	Thos. C. Russell	200	1784		v. 13q, p. 258
69	Conneros Cr.	Lieut. Col. Wm. Scott	450	1784		v. 14q, p. 317
70	Conneros Cr.	John Spence	200	1784		v. 13q, p. 252
71	Conneros Cr.	Jno. Springer	640	1785		v. 6q, p. 374

No.	Location	Name	Acres	Year	Grantee	Reference
72	Conneros Cr.				Robt. Coram	v. 6q, p. 374
73	Conneros Cr.				Peter Gray	v. 6q, p. 374
74	Conneros Cr.				Jas. Kennedy	v. 6q, p. 374
75	Conneros Cr.	Joseph Walker	200	1784		v. 12q, p. 372
76	Conneros Cr.				Jno. Williams	v. 12q, p. 372
77	Conneros Cr.	Lieut. Thos. White	300	1784		v. 14q, p. 327
78	Conneros Cr.	Starret Dobbins	373	1799		v. 37, p. 241
79	Conneros Cr.				Benj. Starrett	v. 37, p. 241
80	Conneros Cr.				M. Glin	v. 37, p. 241
81	26 Mile Cr.	Walter C. Dickson	128	1797		v. 36, p. 107
82	26 Mile Cr.	Abraham Howard	440	1798		v. 37, p. 74
83	26 Mile Cr.				Herrald Filton	v. 37, p. 74
84	26 Mile Cr.	Saml. Beekman	640	1784		v. 5q, p. 34
85	26 Mile Cr.				Jos. Irwin	v. 5q, p. 34
86	26 Mile Cr.	Wm. Beezley	90	1796		v. 33, p. 457
87	26 Mile Cr.				Jas. Saxon	v. 33, p. 457
88	26 Mile Cr.				Henry Peirson	v. 33, p. 457
89	26 Mile Cr.				Jas. Cannon	v. 33, p. 457
90	26 Mile Cr.	Jacob Barr	200	1784		v. 15q, p. 60
91	26 Mile Cr.	John Cannon	200	1786		v. 11q, p. 3
92	26 Mile Cr.	Jacob Capehart	61	1795		v. 32, p. 532
93	26 Mile Cr.				Lewis Jones	v. 32, p. 532
94	26 Mile Cr.				Michael Dickenson	v. 32, p. 532
95	26 Mile Cr.	Edward Camp	288	1785		v. 11q, p. 8
96	26 Mile Cr.				---- Dikison	v. 11q, p. 8
97	26 Mile Cr.	Archibald Campbell	640	1785		v. 5q, p. 52

No.	Stream	Name	Acre	Date	Bounded By	Reference
98	26 Mile Cr.	Tobias Cambridge	640	1784		v. 4q, p. 40
99	26 Mile Cr.	John Calhoun	79	1793		v. 31q, p. 120
100	26 Mile Cr.				----- Faris	v. 31q, p. 120
101	26 Mile Cr.	Thos. Giles	400	1785		v. 13q, p. 205
102	26 Mile Cr.	Alex. Grant	640	1784		v. 5q, p. 107
103	26 Mile Cr.	Jas. Craswell	400	1784		v. 5q, p. 61
104	26 Mile Cr.				Alex. Oliver	v. 5q, p. 61
105	26 Mile Cr.				John Owen	v. 5q, p. 61
106	26 Mile Cr.	John Craig	511	1793		v. 31q, p. 328
107	26 Mile Cr.				----- Turner	v. 31q, p. 328
108	26 Mile Cr.	John Cox	238	1792		v. 31q, p. 24
109	26 Mile Cr.				David Jordon	v. 31q, p. 24
110	26 Mile Cr.				Andrew Liddle	v. 31q, p. 24
111	26 Mile Cr.				John Lince	v. 31q, p. 24
112	26 Mile Cr.				John Morris	v. 31q, p. 24
113	26 Mile Cr.				Henry Pearson	v. 31q, p. 24
114	26 Mile Cr.				James Harris	v. 31q, p. 24
115	26 Mile Cr.	Chichester Curtis	640	1784		v. 5q, p. 63
116	26 Mile Cr.				----- Jones	v. 5q, p. 63
117	26 Mile Cr.	Michael Dickison	333	1785		v. 9q, p. 301
118	26 Mile Cr.				Lewis Jones	v. 9q, p. 301
119	26 Mile Cr.	Wm. Easton	640	1785		v. 4q, p. 154
120	26 Mile Cr.	David Donoon	640	1785		v. 6q, p. 6
121	26 Mile Cr.	Anthony Golding	640	1784		v. 5q, p. 124
122	26 Mile Cr.				----- Findsley	v. 5q, p. 124

No.	Location	Name	Acres	Year		Reference
123	26 Mile Cr.	Archibald Gillison	610	1785		v. 5q, p. 229
124	26 Mile Cr.				Dr. Hall	v. 5q, p. 229
125	26 Mile Cr.	Joseph Hall	640	1784		v. 5q, p. 134
126	26 Mile Cr.	John Hall, Sr.	640	1784		v. 5q, p. 135
127	26 Mile Cr.	Wm. Hairston	308	1785		v. 9q, p. 539
128	26 Mile Cr.				Jas. Cannon	v. 9q, p. 539
129	26 Mile Cr.	Jno. Herriot	640	1785		v. 6q, p. 205
130	26 Mile Cr.	Robert Harper	640	1784		v. 5q, p. 144
131	26 Mile Cr.	Eli Hunecut	482	1785		v. 19q, p. 163
132	26 Mile Cr.				Wm. Brown	v. 19q, p. 163
133	26 Mile Cr.				Lewis Jones	v. 19q, p. 163
134	26 Mile Cr.	Thos. Eveleigh	640	1784		v. 5q, p. 75
135	26 Mile Cr.	Joseph Hutton	224	1793		v. 31, p. 193
136	26 Mile Cr.	Lewis Jones	200	1784		v. 3q, p. 127
137	26 Mile Cr.	Capt. Jno. Joiner	300	1785		v. 15q, p. 91
138	26 Mile Cr.	James Long	400	1784		v. 9q, p. 119
139	26 Mile Cr.				Jno. Owens	v. 9q, p. 119
140	26 Mile Cr.				Alex. Oliver	v. 9q, p. 119
141	26 Mile Cr.	Joseph Martin	360	1784		v. 5q, p. 214
142	26 Mile Cr.	James Milwee	200	1784		v. 9q, p. 409
143	26 Mile Cr.	John Morris	150	1784		v. 8q, p. 149
144	26 Mile Cr.	Edw. Murphey	200	1785		v. 12q, p. 339
145	26 Mile Cr.	John Owen	620	1784		v. 9q, p. 36
146	26 Mile Cr.				Jas. Long	v. 9q, p. 36
147	26 Mile Cr.				Benj. Walley	v. 9q, p. 36
148	26 Mile Cr.				Jas. Little	v. 9q, p. 36

No.	Stream	Name	Acre	Date	Bounded By	Reference
149	26 Mile Cr.	Jas. Patterson	640	1784		v. 15q, p. 156
150	26 Mile Cr.	John Peircy	640	1784		v. 15q, p. 159
151	26 Mile Cr.	James Yancy	400	1786		v. 17q, p. 363
152	26 Mile Cr.	Charles Steel	200	1784		v. 7q, p. 341
153	26 Mile Cr.				Alex. Oliver	v. 7q, p. 341
154	26 Mile Cr.	Wm. Sargeant	640	1784		v. 9q, p. 7
155	26 Mile Cr.	Andrew Liddle	473	1787		v. 21q, p. 217
156	26 Mile Cr.				Francis Gutherie	v. 21q, p. 217
157	26 Mile Cr.	Benj. Waller, Esq.	640	1784		v. 8q, p. 473
158	26 Mile Cr.	Jesse Webb	320	1786		v. 16q, p. 193
159	26 Mile Cr.				Robt. Scott	v. 16q, p. 193
160	26 Mile Cr.	Simeon Doyle	726	1799		v. 37, p. 349
161	26 Mile Cr.				Joseph Case	v. 37, p. 349
162	26 Mile Cr.				----- Cuhen	v. 37, p. 349
163	26 Mile Cr.				----- Turpin	v. 37, p. 349
164	26 Mile Cr.	Walter C. Dickson	128	1797		v. 36, p. 107
165	Hen Coop Cr.	George Reid	320	1784		v. 5q, p. 280
166	Hen Coop Cr.	John Filpot	309	1799		v. 37, p. 342
167	Hen Coop Cr.				Gustin Harris	v. 37, p. 342
168	Hen Coop Cr.				Golman Harris	v. 37, p. 342
169	Hen Coop Cr.				Alex. Snell	v. 37, p. 342
170	Hen Coop Cr.				John Gotcher	v. 37, p. 342
171	Hen Coop Cr.				Chas. Hoynie	v. 37, p. 342
172	Hen Coop Cr.				Jerimiah Morgan	v. 37, p. 342
173	Hen Coop Cr.	Edw. Graham	595	1792		v. 28q, p. 377

No.	Location	Name	Acres	Year	Grantee	Reference
174	Hen Coop Cr.				Peter Frenau	v. 28, p. 377
175	Hen Coop Cr.				Brit. Griffeth	v. 28, p. 377
176	Hen Coop Cr.				----- Broadaway	v. 28q, p. 377
177	Hen Coop Cr.				Prichard Stone	v. 28q, p. 377
178	Hen Coop Cr.				----- Graham	v. 28q, p. 377
179	Hen Coop Cr.	Andrew Lee	100	1784		v. 7q, p. 132
180	Hen Coop Cr.	Daniel Mazyck	640	1784		v. 5q, p. 206
181	Hen Coop Cr.				----- Maxwell	v. 5q, p. 206
182	Hen Coop Cr.	Thomas Jinkins	640	1785		v. 6q, p. 256
183	Hen Coop Cr.	Jas. Gillison	200	1784		v. 5q, p. 300
184	Hen Coop Cr.	Walter Harkins	500	1797		v. 36, p. 139
185	Hen Coop Cr.				Hugh Brown	v. 36, p. 139
186	Hen Coop Cr.				Wm. White	v. 36, p. 139
187	Hen Coop Cr.				Hugh Harkins	v. 36, p. 139
188	Hen Coop Cr.	David Brown	240	1784		v. 9q, p. 526
189	Hen Coop Cr.					v. 9q, p. 526
190	Hen Coop Cr.	Wm. Bennison	712	1790	Jno. Grayson	v. 25q, p. 147
191	Hen Coop Cr.				Jno. Maxwell	v. 25q, p. 147
192	Hen Coop Cr.				Elijah Tuble	v. 25q, p. 147
193	Richland Cr.	Wm. Butler	635	1784		v. 1q, p. 39
194	Richland Cr.				Josiah Allen	v. 1q, p. 39
195	Richland Cr.				Jacob Smith	v. 1q, p. 39
196	Richland Cr.	Capt. Richard Bohun Baker	300	1784		v. 15q, p. 72
197	Richland Cr.	Peter Brooks	330	1785		v. 4q, p. 283
198	Richland Cr.	Capt. Jno. T. Budd	300	1784		v. 15q, p. 64

No.	Stream	Name	Acre	Date	Bounded By	Reference
199	Richland Cr.	Capt. Levacher St. Marie	300	1784		v. 13q, p. 247
200	Richland Cr.	David Goodlett	300	1784		v. 1q, p. 155
201	Richland Cr.	Col. Peter Horry	500	1784		v. 13q, p. 220
202	Richland Cr.	Capt. Wm. Hext	300	1784		v. 13q, p. 228
203	Richland Cr.	Capt. Thos. Shubrick	300	1784		v. 14q, p. 312
204	Richland Cr.	Dr. Fredr. Sunn	300	1784		v. 14q, p. 320
205	Richland Cr.	Elisha Green	148	1799		v. 37, p. 328
206	Richland Cr.				Jesse Carter	v. 37, p. 328
207	Richland Cr.				Jno. Johnston	v. 37, p. 328
208	Richland Cr.				Col. Lemuel Jas Alston	v. 37, p. 328
209	Carpenter Cr.	Abraham Blanding	978	1799		v. 37, p. 396
210	Carpenter Cr.	Jas. Kilgore	330	1796		v. 36, p. 17
211	Carpenter Cr.				Jos. Whitner	v. 36, p. 17
212	Carpenter Cr.				Wm. Bruce	v. 36, p. 17
213	Carpenter Cr.				----- Cunningham	v. 36, p. 17
214	Carpenter Cr.	Nicholas Edwards	150	1785		v. 8q, p. 316
215	Carpenter Cr.				----- Gates	v. 8q, p. 316
216	Carpenter Cr.	Benjamin Stewart	224	1785		v. 20q, p. 104
217	Carpenter Cr.				Robt. McDowell	v. 20q, p. 104
218	Carpenter Cr.	Jas. Gillaspie	330	1796		v. 36, p. 17
219	Carpenter Cr.				Jos. Whitner	v. 36, p. 17
220	Carpenter Cr.				----- Cunningham	v. 36, p. 17
221	Carpenter Cr.				Wm. Bruce	v. 36, p. 17
222	Cane Cr.	John Adair & James Curry	339	1793		v. 29q, p. 116

223	Cane Cr.	James Courtney	500	1798		v. 37, p. 85
224	Cane Cr.				Wm. Bozley	v. 37, p. 85
225	Cane Cr.	Jacob Clearman	500	1799		v. 37, p. 345
226	Cane Cr.				Presly Self	v. 37, p. 345
227	Cane Cr.	Elloner Brooks	223	1786		v. 19q, p. 188
228	Cane Cr.	Jean Brown	250	1784		v. 9q, p. 372
229	Cane Cr.				Jno. Hawkins	v. 9q, p. 372
230	Cane Cr.	John Butler	200	1784		v. 4q, p. 295
231	Cane Cr.				Walter Burrel	v. 4q, p. 295
232	Cane Cr.				Davis Grimes	v. 4q, p. 295
233	Cane Cr.				Daniel Hail	v. 4q, p. 295
234	Cane Cr.	Duncan Bryan	330	1787		v. 16q, p. 304
235	Cane Cr.				Jno. Philpot	v. 16q, p. 304
236	Cane Cr.				Jas. White	v. 16q, p. 304
237	Cane Cr.				Sam Hall	v. 16q, p. 304
238	Cane Cr.	Samuel Cobb	731	1793		v. 31q, p. 326
239	Cane Cr.	Joshua Eckols	282	1793		v. 31q, p. 240
240	Cane Cr.				Pendleton Isbell	v. 31q, p. 240
241	Cane Cr.	Major Isaac Harlston	400	1784		v. 13q, p. 240
242	Cane Cr.	Wm. Farmer	200	1786		v. 15q, p. 343
243	Cane Cr.	Potter Inlow	192	1784		v. 3q, p. 286
244	Cane Cr.				Jas. Hawkins	v. 3q, p. 286
245	Cane Cr.	Charley Plunket	123	1793		v. 29q, p. 331
246	Cane Cr.	Anthony Griffin	400	1797		v. 36, p. 53
247	Cane Cr.				Jas. Yowel	v. 36, p. 53
248	Cane Cr.				Jas. Divenport	v. 36, p. 53

No.	Stream	Name	Acre	Date	Bounded By	Reference
249	Cane Cr.				Wm. Steele	v. 36, p. 53
250	Cane Cr.	Wm. Gray	273	1797		v. 36, p. 58
251	Cane Cr.				Reuben Tile	v. 36, p. 58
252	Oo lenoy Cr.	William Lynch	328	1798		v. 37, p. 68
253	Oo lenoy Cr.				----- Moore	v. 37, p. 68
254	Oo lenoy Cr.				Peter Perkins	v. 37, p. 68
255	Oo lenoy Cr.	Wm. Reighty	340	1784		v. 5q, p. 298
256	Oo lenoy Cr.	Saml. Weaver	100	1784		v. 3q, p. 275
257	Oo lenoy Cr.	Alex. Edens	496	1798		v. 37, p. 39
258	Oo lenoy Cr.				Jas. Davis	v. 37, p. 39
259	Oo lenoy Cr.	William Glenn	480	1799		v. 37, p. 243
260	Oo lenoy Cr.				Saml. Watts	v. 37, p. 243
261	Oo lenoy Cr.				Isaac Davis	v. 37, p. 243
262	Oo lenoy Cr.	Richard Bell	143	1786		v. 18q, p. 91
263	Oo lenoy Cr.	Samuel Hand	411	1797		v. 36, p. 164
264	Oo lenoy Cr.				Major Vanderhort	v. 36, p. 164
265	Oo lenoy Cr.				Wm. Ryley	v. 36, p. 164
266	Oo lenoy Cr.	Edw. Chastain	150	1796		v. 32, p. 571
267	Oo lenoy Cr.	William Blyth	114	1785		v. 9q, p. 351
268	Oo lenoy Cr.				Benj. Clark	v. 9q, p. 351
269	Oo lenoy Cr.	Mary Creswell	200	1784		v. 1q, p. 95
270	Oo lenoy Cr.				Jno. Norwood	v. 1q, p. 95
271	Oo lenoy Cr.	James Davis	250	1784		v. 1q, p. 124
272	Oo lenoy Cr.	John Fatheree	640	1784		v. 5q, p. 73
273	18 Mile Cr.	Jno. Anderson	200	1785		v. 13q, p. 13

No.	Location	Name	Acres	Year	Grantee	Reference
274	18 Mile Cr.	Harry Person	158	1785		v. 15q, p. 99
275	18 Mile Cr.				Thos. Hulom	v. 15q, p. 99
276	18 Mile Cr.				Wm. Hulom	v. 15q, p. 99
277	18 Mile Cr.	Wm. Hamilton	420	1798		v. 37, p. 121
278	18 Mile Cr.				Wm. Wallace	v. 37, p. 121
279	18 Mile Cr.	Geo. Beneson	200	1784		v. 10q, p. 38
280	18 Mile Cr.				Peter Sinkler	v. 10q, p. 38
281	18 Mile Cr.	Jacob Berkley	640	1785		v. 8q, p. 500
282	18 Mile Cr.				Jno. Martin	v. 8q, p. 500
283	18 Mile Cr.				David Hamilton	v. 8q, p. 500
284	18 Mile Cr.				Bizzel Hallum	v. 8q, p. 500
285	18 Mile Cr.	Jas. Bowling	200	1787		v. 14q, p. 233
286	18 Mile Cr.				Locklen Leonard	v. 14q, p. 233
287	18 Mile Cr.	Wm. Burney	1000	1792		v. 26q, p. 335
288	18 Mile Cr.				Thos. Hughes	v. 26q, p. 355
289	18 Mile Cr.				Thos. Gadson	v. 26q, p. 355
290	18 Mile Cr.				Ephriam Lindsey	v. 26q, p. 355
291	18 Mile Cr.	Jno. Caldwell	306	1792		v. 28q, p. 282
292	18 Mile Cr.				Chas. Hughes	v. 28q, p. 282
293	18 Mile Cr.				Thos. Boyd	v. 28q, p. 282
294	18 Mile Cr.	Jno. Currell	200	1784		v. 13q, p. 109
295	18 Mile Cr.	Saml. Henry Dickson	386	1788		v. 23q, p. 375
296	18 Mile Cr.				Jno. Martin	v. 23q, p. 375
297	18 Mile Cr.				Mary Leonard	v. 23q, p. 375
298	18 Mile Cr.	Ambrose Dedley	173	1795		v. 32, p. 498
299	18 Mile Cr.				Jno. Hallum	v. 32, p. 498

No.	Stream	Name	Acre	Date	Bounded By	Reference
300	18 Mile Cr.	Henry Ellis			Andrew Pickens	v. 32, p. 498
301	18 Mile Cr.		640	1785		v. 5q, p. 76
302	18 Mile Cr.				Jacob Berkley	v. 5q, p. 76
303	18 Mile Cr.				Jas. Elsinore	v. 5q, p. 76
304	18 Mile Cr.	Lewis Gervais, Esq.	640	1784		v. 4q, p. 122
305	18 Mile Cr.	David Hamilton	200	----		v. 4q, p. 196
306	18 Mile Cr.	Bazzel Hallum	380	1785		v. 4q, p. 190
307	18 Mile Cr.				Henry Goucher	v. 4q, p. 190
308	18 Mile Cr.	Jno. Jackson	640	1785		v. 4q, p. 136
309	18 Mile Cr.				Jno. Fearson	v. 4q, p. 136
310	18 Mile Cr.				Robt Lusk	v. 4q, p. 136
311	18 Mile Cr.	Jno. Hunter, Esq.	300	1784		v. 10q, p. 167
312	18 Mile Cr.	Isaac Lynch	398	1787		v. 19q, p. 328
313	18 Mile Cr.				Chas. Seys	v. 19q, p. 328
314	18 Mile Cr.				Jno. Miller	v. 19q, p. 328
315	18 Mile Cr.				Isaac Titsworth	v. 19q, p. 328
316	18 Mile Cr.				D. Brag	v. 19q, p. 328
317	18 Mile Cr.	Lachlin Leonard	200	1786		v. 14q, p. 266
318	18 Mile Cr.				Mary Leonard	v. 14q, p. 266
319	18 Mile Cr.	Jas. Nevin	200	1784		v. 12q, p. 155
320	18 Mile Cr.	Jos. Scarff	200	1784		v. 12q, p. 310
321	18 Mile Cr.	Peter Sinkler	640	1784		v. 9q, p. 48
322	18 Mile Cr.				Geo. Kelson	v. 9q, p. 48
323	18 Mile Cr.	Jas. Waddle	200	1784		v. 12q, p. 336
324	18 Mile Cr.	Jos. Whitner	427	1785		v. 4q, p. 433

No.	Location	Grantee	Acres	Year	Other Name	Reference
325	18 Mile Cr.	Benj. Wood	200	1784		v. 12q, p. 318
326	18 Mile Cr.				Fredk. Ellick	v. 12q, p. 318
327	18 Mile Cr.	Jno. Woodside	400	1789		v. 27q, p. 219
328	18 Mile Cr.				Wm. Swift	v. 27q, p. 219
329	Lit. Generostee Cr.					
330	"	William Adams	250	1784		v. 4q, p. 361
331	"	James Dickey	44	1798		v. 37, p. 105
332	"				Jas. Hammoger	v. 37, p. 105
333	"				Wm. Simpson	v. 37, p. 105
334	"				Jas. Watts	v. 37, p. 105
335	"				Jno. Hamilton	v. 37, p. 105
336	"	Jacob Drayton	640	1784	Wm. Adams	v. 37, p. 105
337	"	Danl. Gellespie	300	1785		v. 6q, p. 4
338	"	Jas. Hammenger	200	1784		v. 11q, p. 339
339	"				Jno. Hamilton	v. 15q, p. 98
340	"				Jno. Weslley	v. 15q, p. 98
341	"				And. Pickens	v. 15q, p. 98
342	"	Jno. Hamilton	300	1784		v. 4q, p. 161
343	"	James Watt	196	1785		v. 16q, p. 188
344	"					v. 16q, p. 188
345	"	Alex. Young	200	1784	Andw. Young	v. 8q, p. 194
346	Big Generostee Cr.	Francis Albertia	640	1784		v. 2q, p. 239
347	"	Jas. Alexander	200	1785		v. 7q, p. 398
348	"	Asaph Alexander	200	1784		v. 2q, p. 245

No.	Stream	Name	Acre	Date	Bounded By	Reference
349	Big Generostee Cr.	Arthur Durley	248	1798		v. 37, p. 131
350	"				Bartholomew White	v. 37, p. 131
351	"				Jno. Martin	v. 37, p. 131
352	"				Jno. Smith	v. 37, p. 131
353	"				Jno. Durley	v. 37, p. 131
354	"				Jos. Land	v. 37, p. 131
355	"	Robt. Peacock	200	1785		v. 15q, p. 314
356	"	Peter Kays	403	1797		v. 36, p. 80
357	"				Jno. Moore	v. 36, p. 80
358	"				Jno. Smith	v. 36, p. 80
359	"	Jas. Anderson	320	1784		v. 4q, p. 88
360	"	Jno. Beech	640	1784		v. 15q, p. 33
361	"	Jno. Boles	188	1785		v. 2q, p. 172
362	"				Gilly Mills	v. 2q, p. 172
363	"	Jas. Blythe	640	1784		v. 10q, p. 41
364	"	Elloner Black	472	1785		v. 15q, p. 10
365	"				Isaac Steel	v. 15q, p. 10
366	"	Jas. Brock	200	1784		v. 3q, p. 13
367	"	Joel Bratcher	223	1789		v. 24q, p. 23
368	"	Daniel Cross	640	1784		v. 5q, p. 59
369	"	Josiah East	270	1785		v. 9q, p. 362
370	"	Thos. Dranan	235	1792		v. 28q, p. 264
371	"				Thos. Wadsworth	v. 28q, p. 264
372	"				Joshua Saxon	v. 28q, p. 264

No.	Location	Name		Acres	Year	Reference
373	"	Jno. Gabriel		186	1788	v. 23q, p. 365
374	"	Andw. Hamilton		150	1784	v. 3q, p. 78
375	"	Elijah Herrin		12	1793	v. 31q, p. 178
376	"		Saml. Dalrymple			v. 31q, p. 178
377	"		Henry Pearson			v. 31q, p. 178
378	"	Saml. Haston		200	1784	v. 8q, p. 176
379	"	Abslom Hervey		640	1785	v. 1q, p. 380
380	"		Wm. Hampton			v. 1q, p. 380
381	"	Jno. Johnson		640	1785	v. 1q, p. 402
382	"	Aeson Jay		254	1786	v. 21q, p. 202
383	"	Danl. McCollum		400	1786	v. 18q, p. 158
384	"		Jas. Jordan			v. 18q, p. 158
385	"	Gilbert Mills		200	1786	v. 14q, p. 272
386	"		Jno. McCarter			v. 14q, p. 272
387	"	Wm. Morrel		259	1789	v. 24q, p. 234
388	"	Thos. Moss		170	1786	v. 17q, p. 173
389	"	Jno. Parker		640	1784	v. 16q, p. 226
390	"	Wm. Parsons		300	1785	v. 14q, p. 305
391	"	Jos. H. Ramsay		640	1784	v. 5q, p. 391
392	"	Wm. Searight		384	1785	v. 5q, p. 380
393	"	David Shadden		640	1784	v. 9q, p. 106
394	"	Jas. Simpson		223	1785	v. 17q, p. 32
395	"	John Smith		640	1784	v. 9q, p. 139
396	"	Isaac Steel		68	1785	v. 7q, p. 411
397	"		Thos. Lesley			v. 7q, p. 411
398	Tugaloo Riv.	Aaron Smith		200	1784	v. 13q, p. 254

47

No.	Stream	Name	Acre	Date	Bounded By	Reference
399	Tugaloo Riv.	Joshua Eckols	359	1797	Hugh Milling	v. 13q, p. 254
400	Tugaloo Riv.					v. 36, p. 56
401	Tugaloo Riv.				Lewis Rolston	v. 36, p. 56
402	Tugaloo Riv.	Garret Fitzgerrel	425	1797		v. 36, p. 140
403	Tugaloo Riv.				Jesse Caffee	v. 36, p. 140
404	Tugaloo Riv.				Ambrose Fitzgerrel	v. 37, p. 140
405	Tugaloo Riv.	Ambrose Fitzgerrel	71	1799		v. 37, p. 217
406	Tugaloo Riv.				Garret Fitzgarrel	v. 37, p. 217
407	Tugaloo Riv.				Aaron Terrel	v. 37, p. 217
408	Tugaloo Riv.				Wm. Boyd	v. 37, p. 217
409	Tugaloo Riv.	Michael Hutchins	212	1797		v. 36, p. 119
410	Tugaloo Riv.				Jno. Robison	v. 36q, p. 119
411	Tugaloo Riv.	Ezekiel Adams	200	1784		v. 15q, p. 76
412	Tugaloo Riv.				Jno. Humphrey	v. 15q, p. 76
413	Tugaloo Riv.				Jno. Muleaston	v. 15q, p. 76
414	Tugaloo Riv.	Jno. Chavees	200	1784		v. 13q, p. 167
415	Tugaloo Riv.	Wm. Cleveland	290	1794		v. 33, p. 30
416	Tugaloo Riv.				Gideon Clark	v. 33, p. 30
417	Tugaloo Riv.				Jas. Bryant	v. 33, p. 30
418	Tugaloo Riv.				Larkin Cleveland	v. 33, p. 30
419	Tugaloo Riv.	Wm. Clark	52	1787		v. 24q, p. 45
420	Tugaloo Riv.	Jas. Crawford	325	1795		v. 32, p. 526
421	Tugaloo Riv.				Aaron Smith	v. 32, p. 526
422	Tugaloo Riv.				Lewis Shilton	v. 32, p. 526
423	Tugaloo Riv.	Jno. Cleveland	290	1788		v. 23q, p. 159

No.	Location	Grantee	Acres	Year	Adjacent	Reference
424	Tugaloo Riv.				Thos. Cox	v. 23q, p. 159
425	Tugaloo Riv.	Thos. Cox	56	1787		v. 21q, p. 139
426	Tugaloo Riv.				Capt. Blackburn	v. 21q, p. 139
427	Tugaloo Riv.				Saml. Taylor	v. 21q, p. 139
428	Tugaloo Riv.	Reuben Denton	200	1784		v. 13q, p. 240
429	Tugaloo Riv.				Jno. Smith	v. 13q, p. 240
430	Tugaloo Riv.	Wm. Emmerson	90	1791		v. 27q, p. 487
431	Tugaloo Riv.				Benj. Cleveland	v. 27q, p. 487
432	Tugaloo Riv.	Wm. Guest	690	1787		v. 22q, p. 32
433	Tugaloo Riv.	Gilbert Grooms	200	1784		v. 13q, p. 212
434	Tugaloo Riv.				Jno. Goodwyn	v. 13q, p. 212
435	Tugaloo Riv.				Jno. Smith	v. 13q, p. 212
436	Tugaloo Riv.	Jno. McGee	200	1784		v. 14q, p. 300
437	Tugaloo Riv.	Major Parsons	65	1785		v. 9q, p. 415
438	Tugaloo Riv.	Capt. Thos. Weaver	300	1784		v. 14q, p. 326
439	Lit. Eastatoe	Elias Earle	435	1797		v. 36, p. 137
440	Lit. Eastatoe	James Smith	640	1784		v. 10q, p. 69
441	Lit. Eastatoe	Isaac Gilder	65	1791		v. 27q, p. 268
442	Lit. Eastatoe				Wm. Bruce	v. 27q, p. 268
443	Lit. Eastatoe				Jno. Young	v. 27q, p. 268
444	Lit. Eastatoe	Albert F. Smithson	300	1788		v. 25q, p. 234
445	Lit. Eastatoe	Thos. Beard	85	1799		v. 37, p. 246
446	Big Eastatoe	James Clark	822	1799		v. 37, p. 403
447	Big Eastatoe				Henry Terrel	v. 37, p. 403
448	Big Eastatoe				Simon & Deyer	v. 37, p. 403
449	Big Eastatoe	Micajah Clark	269	1799		v. 37, p. 404

No.	Stream	Name	Acre	Date	Bounded By	Reference
450	Big Eastatoe	Adam Right	640	1784	Mashack Stevens	v. 37, p. 404
451	Big Eastatoe	Amanatious Thomas	335	1785		v. 5q, p. 337
452	Big Eastatoe	Jerimiah Fields	500	1799		v. 1q, p. 149
453	Big Eastatoe	Joshua Dyer	100	1793		v. 37, p. 401
454	Big Eastatoe	Geo. Naylor	1000	1794		v. 31, p. 291
455	Big Eastatoe					v. 32, p. 291
456	Big Eastatoe				Robt. Middleton	v. 32, p. 291
457	Big Eastatoe	James Jett	979	1799		v. 37, p. 402
458	Big Eastatoe				Jno. Simmons	v. 37, p. 402
459	23 Mile Cr.	Thomas Abett	315	1785		v. 11q, p. 148
460	23 Mile Cr.	Bennett Aden	500	1796		v. 33q, p. 455
461	23 Mile Cr.	Simeon Dyole	726	1799		v. 37, p. 349
462	23 Mile Cr.				----- Cuhen	v. 37, p. 349
463	23 Mile Cr.				Jos. Case	v. 37, p. 349
464	23 Mile Cr.				----- Turpin	v. 37, p. 349
465	23 Mile Cr.	Saml. H. Dickson	177	1797		v. 36, p. 148
466	23 Mile Cr.				Abner Hale	v. 36, p. 148
467	23 Mile Cr.				Stephen Wadsworth	v. 36, p. 148
468	23 Mile Cr.				Thos. Wadsworth	v. 36, p. 148
469	23 Mile Cr.				Lydia Maverick	v. 36, p. 148
470	23 Mile Cr.	Jacob Phillips	26	1792		v. 31q, p. 61
471	23 Mile Cr.				Jno. Robertson	v. 31q, p. 61
472	23 Mile Cr.				Wm. Boyce	v. 31q, p. 61
473	23 Mile Cr.	Ezekiel Pilgrim	300	1784		v. 17q, p. 329
474	23 Mile Cr.				Jas. Liddle	v. 17q, p. 329

475	23 Mile Cr.	Alex. Robeson	640	1784		v. 9q, p. 78
476	23 Mile Cr.	Jno. Robinson, Jr.	150	1784		v. 8q, p. 4
478	23 Mile Cr.				Thos. Wadsworth	v. 8q, p. 4
479	23 Mile Cr.	Chas. Saxon	200	1785		v. 3q, p. 190
480	23 Mile Cr.	Benj. Smith	250	1784		v. 10q, p. 72
481	23 Mile Cr.	Susannah Wadsworth	300	1784		v. 12q, p. 329
482	23 Mile Cr.				Sofia Caise	v. 12q, p. 329
483	23 Mile Cr.	Andw. Warnock	200	1784		v. 7q, p. 320
484	23 Mile Cr.	Saml. H. Dickson	177	1797		v. 36, p. 148
485	23 Mile Cr.				Abner Steele	v. 36, p. 148
486	23 Mile Cr.				Stephen Wadsworth	v. 36, p. 148
487	23 Mile Cr.				Thos. Wadsworth	v. 36, p. 148
488	23 Mile Cr.				Lydia Maverick	v. 36, p. 148
489	23 Mile Cr.	Britain George	120	1796		v. 36, p. 14
490	23 Mile Cr.				Hugh Wornich	v. 36, p. 14
491	23 Mile Cr.				David Smith	v. 36, p. 14
492	23 Mile Cr.	Philip Gadsden	640	1784		v. 6q, p. 217
493	23 Mile Cr.				Gen. Pinckney	v. 6q, p. 217
494	23 Mile Cr.				Ephraim Lindsey	v. 6q, p. 217
495	23 Mile Cr.	Peter Frenau	640	1786		v. 10q, p. 222
496	23 Mile Cr.	James Hacket	640	1784		v. 5q, p. 131
497	23 Mile Cr.	Thos. Davidson	191	1787		v. 20q, p. 249
498	23 Mile Cr.				Benj. Bowars	v. 20q, p. 249
499	23 Mile Cr.	James Dutilly	640	1784		v. 5q, p. 90
500	23 Mile Cr.	Thos. Dunbar	200	1785		v. 13q, p. 200
501	23 Mile Cr.	John Drennan	200	1785		v. 17q, p. 368

51

No.	Stream	Name	Acre	Date	Bounded By	Reference
502	23 Mile Cr.	Saml. Norwood	300	1784		v. 15q, p. 267
503	23 Mile Cr.	Jas. Martin	180	1784		v. 5q, p. 222
504	23 Mile Cr.				Jas. Liddle	v. 5q, p. 222
505	23 Mile Cr.	Lydia Maverick	640	1784		v. 5q, p. 210
506	23 Mile Cr.	Jno. Moore	200	1786		v. 12q, p. 76
507	23 Mile Cr.				Francis Benneau	v. 12q, p. 76
508	23 Mile Cr.	Ruber Goulden	200	1786		v. 22q, p. 241
509	23 Mile Cr.				David Smith	v. 22q, p. 241
510	23 Mile Cr.	Isham Irby	499	1796		v. 32, p. 644
511	23 Mile Cr.				Alex. Powers	v. 32, p. 644
512	23 Mile Cr.	Henry Hunter	640	1784		v. 4q, p. 150
513	23 Mile Cr.	Gabriel Harden	319	1790		v. 25q, p. 100
514	23 Mile Cr.				Andw. Rowe	v. 25q, p. 100
515	23 Mile Cr.				Jas. Jenkins	v. 25q, p. 100
516	23 Mile Cr.	Bowling Clark	320	1784		v. 4q, p. 224
517	23 Mile Cr.	Saml. Chapman	249	1795		v. 32, p. 454
518	23 Mile Cr.				Henry Dobson	v. 32, p. 454
519	23 Mile Cr.	Thos. Abett	315	1785		v. 11q, p. 148
520	23 Mile Cr.				Jonothan Clark	v. 11q, p. 148
521	23 Mile Cr.	Leonard Boone	462	1795		v. 32, p. 449
522	23 Mile Cr.	Francis Bonneau	640	1784		v. 10q, p. 46
523	23 Mile Cr.	Wm. Hodges	190	1785		v. 9q, p. 336
524	23 Mile Cr.	Abigail Johnson	471	1785		v. 2q, p. 307
525	23 Mile Cr.				----- Smith	v. 2q, p. 307

No.	Location	Grantee	Acres	Year	Name	Reference
526	23 Mile Cr.				----- Willimon	v. 2q, p. 307
527	23 Mile Cr.				----- Willson	v. 2q, p. 307
528	23 Mile Cr.	Bennett Aden	500	1796		v. 33, p. 455
529	23 Mile Cr.				Wm. Macky	v. 33, p. 455
530	23 Mile Cr.				Eliz. Robinson	v. 33, p. 455
531	23 Mile Cr.				----- Stephen	v. 33, p. 455
532	23 Mile Cr.	Benj. Call	640	1784		v. 4q, p. 44
533	23 Mile Cr.				Henry Hunter	v. 4q, p. 44
534	23 Mile Cr.	Capt. Jno. Calhoun	300	1784		v. 4q, p. 14
535	23 Mile Cr.				Andw. Warnock	v. 4q, p. 14
536	23 Mile Cr.	Wm. Hamilton	173	1798		v. 37, p. 112
537	23 Mile Cr.				Wm. Forbes	v. 37, p. 112
538	23 Mile Cr.				Wm. Wallace	v. 37, p. 112
539	23 Mile Cr.				Thos. Hamilton	v. 37, p. 112
540	12 Mile Cr.	Bayley Anderson	424	1793		v. 29q, p. 115
541	12 Mile Cr.	Jno. Bynum	567	1799		v. 37, p. 460
542	12 Mile Cr.	Job Barnard	100	1790		v. 25q, p. 340
543	12 Mile Cr.				Baily Anderson	v. 25q, p. 340
544	12 Mile Cr.	Jno. Robertson	640	1784		v. 9q, p. 63
545	12 Mile Cr.	Geo. Robuck	440	1786		v. 14q, p. 130
546	12 Mile Cr.	Thos. Stewart	640	1784		v. 8q, p. 455
546	12 Mile Cr.	Jno. Tenison	93	1789		v. 24q, p. 358
548	12 Mile Cr.	Jos. Duncan	82	1797		v. 36, p. 162
549	12 Mile Cr.				Jno. Gowan	v. 36, p. 162
550	12 Mile Cr.	Jesse Ellis	467	1797		v. 36, p. 134
551	12 Mile Riv.				Wm. Binson	v. 36, p. 134

53

No.	Stream	Name	Acre	Date	Bounded By	Reference
552	12 Mile Riv.				Wm. Bynum	v. 36, p. 134
553	12 Mile Riv.				Isaac Bynum	v. 36, p. 134
554	12 Mile Riv.				Jos. Duncan	v. 36, p. 134
555	12 Mile Riv.	Robt. Fullerton	500	1798		v. 36, p. 169
556	12 Mile Riv.				Gen. Anderson	v. 36, p. 169
557	12 Mile Riv.				Jos. Smith	v. 36, p. 169
558	12 Mile Riv.	Jno. Caruther	344	1785		v. 13q, p. 121
559	12 Mile Riv.	Ulrig Carpenter	112	1785		v. 14q, p. 159
560	12 Mile Riv.	Jno. Black	212	1785		v. 9q, p. 291
561	12 Mile Riv.	Jos. French	72	1790		v. 25q, p. 36
562	12 Mile Riv.				----- Salmon	v. 25q, p. 36
563	12 Mile Riv.				----- Young	v. 25q, p. 36
564	12 Mile Riv.	Jno. Gowen	294	1785		v. 11q, p. 328
565	12 Mile Riv.				Enoch Hooper	v. 11q, p. 328
566	12 Mile Riv.	Saml. Earle, Esq.	150	1786		v. 11q, p. 126
567	12 Mile Riv.	Jos. Duncan	355	1791		v. 28q, p. 30
568	12 Mile Riv.	Wm. Murphree	439	1790		v. 27q, p. 75
569	12 Mile Riv.	Thos. Potter	100	1785		v. 8q, p. 335
570	12 Mile Riv.	Benj. Ingram	640	1786		v. 13q, p. 173
571	12 Mile Riv.				Jas. Ferguson	v. 13q, p. 173
572	12 Mile Riv.	Jos. Henderson	325	1785		v. 9q, p. 426
573	12 Mile Riv.				Enoch Hooper	v. 9q, p. 426
574	12 Mile Riv.	Patrick Hays	640	1784		v. 5q, p. 151
575	12 Mile Riv.	Joel Haulcom	290	1786		v. 13q, p. 32
576	12 Mile Riv.				----- Woodal	v. 13q, p. 32

No.	Location	Name	Acres	Year	Second Name	Reference
577	12 Mile Riv.	Henry Chiles	150	1785		v. 11q, p. 154
578	12 Mile Riv.	Francis Boren	66	1793		v. 29q, p. 30
579	12 Mile Riv.				Amos Freman	v. 29q, p. 30
580	12 Mile Riv.				Baylis Earle	v. 29q, p. 30
581	12 Mile Riv.	Jno. Huggins	200	1785		v. 14q, p. 260
582	12 Mile Riv.	Maurica Casedy	640	1784		v. 4q, p. 68
583	12 Mile Riv.	Alex. Burns	214	1793		v. 31q, p. 222
584	12 Mile Riv.				Wm. Thompson	v. 31q, p. 222
585	12 Mile Riv.				----- Bobo	v. 31q, p. 222
586	12 Mile Riv.				------ Murphree	v. 31q, p. 222
587	12 Mile Riv.	Job Barnard	100	1790		v. 25q, p. 340
588	12 Mile Riv.				Bailey Anderson	v. 25q, p. 340
589	12 Mile Riv.				----- Hill	v. 25q, p. 340
590	12 Mile Riv.	Bradford Camp	134	1788		v. 23q, p. 243
591	12 Mile Riv.	Duncan Cammeron	189	1786		v. 16q, p. 21
592	12 Mile Riv.	Jno. Ewing Calhoun Esq.	400	1785		v. 1q, p. 306
593	12 Mile Riv.	Jno. Hudson, Sr.	350	1799		v. 37, p. 244
594	12 Mile Riv.				----- Young	v. 37, p. 244
595	12 Mile Riv.				----- Silman	v. 37, p. 244
596	Choestoe Cr.	Lieut. Nath. Bradwell	200	1784		v. 15q, p. 65
597	Choestoe Cr.	Lewis Davis	139	1788		v. 23q, p. 336
598	Choestoe Cr.				Saml. Lofton	v. 23q, p. 336
599	Choestoe Cr.	Harmin Davis	300	1784		v. 13q, p. 198
600	Choestoe Cr.	Jno. Lewis	190	1788		v. 23q, p. 334
601	Choestoe Cr.				Saml. Loston	v. 23q, p. 334
602	Choestoe Cr.	Joshua Lee	354	1787		v. 19q, p. 203

No.	Stream	Name	Acre	Date	Bounded By	Reference
603	Choestoe Cr.	Benj. Jones	200	1784		v. 15q, p. 84
604	Choestoe Cr.	Wm. Dickson	105	1801		v. 38, p. 332
605	Choestoe Cr.	Reuben Simpson	427	1792		v. 28q, p. 129
606	Choestoe Cr.				Solomon White	v. 28q, p. 129
607	Choestoe Cr.				Wm. McCalip	v. 28q, p. 129
608	Choestoe Cr.				Nat. Perry	v. 28q, p. 129
609	Choestoe Cr.	Jno. Skelton	200	1784		v. 14q, p. 317
610	Choestoe Cr.	Eli Davis	47	1798		v. 36, p. 177
611	Choestoe Cr.				Saml. Burton	v. 36, p. 177
612	Choestoe Cr.				Nathl. Perry	v. 36, p. 177
613	Wilson's Cr.	Geo. Craswell	300	1785		v. 6q, p. 109
614	Wilson's Cr.				David Jordon	v. 6q, p. 109
615	Wilson's Cr.				Jno. Parker	v. 6q, p. 109
616	Wilson's Cr.	Jas. McAdoo	340	1785		v. 17q, p. 101
617	Wilson's Cr.				Wm. Bears	v. 17q, p. 101
618	Wilson's Cr.	Alex. Noble	150	1784		v. 10q, p. 472
619	Wilson's Cr.				Andw. Norris	v. 10q, p. 472
620	Wilson's Cr.	Ezekiel Evans	434	1791		v. 27q, p. 473
621	Wilson's Cr.	Wm. Ebenezer Kennedy	640	1795		v. 27q, p. 404
622	Wilson's Cr.	Wm. Thompson	425	1786		v. 16q, p. 369
623	Seneca Riv.	Jas. Bole	500	1798		v. 37, p. 98
624	Seneca Riv.	Joel Ledbetter	222	1798		v. 37, p. 15
625	Seneca Riv.				David Gillespie	v. 37, p. 15
626	Seneca Riv.				Jno. Cannon	v. 37, p. 15
627	Seneca Riv.				----- Stephenson	v. 37, p. 15
628	Seneca Riv.				Chas. Heargraves	v. 37, p. 15

No.	Location	Name	Acres	Year	Name 2	Reference
629	Seneca Riv.	Wm. Gabriel Pickens	200	1784		v. 17q, p. 248
630	Seneca Riv.	Jas. Tate, Sr.	320	1784		v. 5q, p. 198
631	Seneca Riv.				Robt. Tate	v. 5q, p. 198
632	Toxaway Riv.	Jno. Calvert	200	1795		v. 32, p. 418
633	Toxaway Riv.	Jacob Faust	146	1799		v. 37, p. 315
634	Toxaway Riv.				Chas. Baker	v. 37, p. 315
635	Toxaway Riv.				Jos. Step	v. 37, p. 315
636	Toxaway Riv.				Danl. McMillon	v. 37, p. 315
637	Toxaway Riv.				Chas. Kennedy	v. 37, p. 315
638	Wolf Cr.	Jno. Bynum	500	1798		v. 37, p. 63
639	Wolf Cr.	Jos. Duncan	268	1797		v. 36, p. 161
640	Wolf Cr.				Wm. Bynum	v. 36, p. 161
641	Wolf Cr.				Levi Murphree	v. 36, p. 161
642	Wolf Cr.				Jas. Jett	v. 36, p. 161
643	Wolf Cr.	Willis Benson	342	1785		v. 4q, p. 397
644	Wolf Cr.				Jas. Henderson	v. 4q, p. 397
645	Wolf Cr.	David Henderson	156	1785		v. 11q, p. 185
646	Wolf Cr.	Mathew Gillespie	154	1785		v. 14q, p. 23
647	Wolf Cr.	Benj. Perry	640	1785		v. 17q, p. 279
648	Wolf Cr.				Jas. Bruce	v. 17q, p. 279
649	Georges Cr.	Lewis Dinkins	500	1798		v. 37, p. 84
650	Georges Cr.				Robt. Easley	v. 37, p. 84
651	Georges Cr.				Jno. Carew	v. 37, p. 84
652	Georges Cr.				----- Sadler	v. 37, p. 84
653	Georges Cr.				Wade & Fleming	v. 37, p. 84
654	Georges Cr.	Michael Boulger	500	1798		v. 37, p. 85

No.	Stream	Name	Acre	Date	Bounded By	Reference
655	Georges Cr.	Zephimah Roberts	150	1784		v. 8q, p. 6
656	Georges Cr.				Jno. McMahan	v. 8q, p. 6
657	Georges Cr.				Wm. McCaleb	v. 8q, p. 6
658	Georges Cr.	Hugh Rose	640	1784		v. 16q, p. 269
659	Georges Cr.				Ephriam Mitchel	v. 16q, p. 269
660	Georges Cr.				Zeph. Roberts	v. 16q, p. 269
661	Georges Cr.	Jno. Swords	640	1784		v. 5q, p. 374
662	Georges Cr.	James Jones	206	1790		v. 25q, p. 219
663	Georges Cr.				Chas. Smith	v. 25q, p. 219
664	Georges Cr.	Francis Lay	200	1788		v. 21q, p. 340
665	Georges Cr.				Jno. Hallum	v. 21q, p. 340
666	Georges Cr.	Wm. Hallum	300	1784		v. 4q, p. 169
667	Georges Cr.	Joel Callahan	300	1785		v. 9q, p. 294
668	Georges Cr.				Jacob Vance	v. 9q, p. 294
669	Georges Cr.	Jno. Callahan	300	1785		v. 6q, p. 145
670	Georges Cr.				Joel Callahan	v. 6q, p. 145
671	Georges Cr.	Robt. Bowan	289	1786		v. 19q, p. .31
672	Georges Cr.	Thos. Boyd	147	1796		v. 32, p. 604
673	Georges Cr.				----- Gillaspie	v. 32, p. 604
674	Georges Cr.				----- Bowan	v. 32, p. 604
675	Georges Cr.				----- Rowland	v. 32, p. 604
676	Georges Cr.				----- Hallum	v. 32, p. 604
677	Georges Cr.	Jno. Boyd	1761	1786		v. 19q, p. 17
678	Georges Cr.				----- Gillaspie	v. 19q, p. 17
679	Georges Cr.	Wm. Bead	606	1785		v. 19q, p. 259

No.	Location	Name	Acres	Year	Adjoining	Reference
680	Georges Cr.	Jno. Hood	268	1797		v. 36, p. 47
681	Georges Cr.		178	1791	Jno. Boyd	v. 36, p. 47
682	Georges Cr.	Jno. Armstrong				v. 27q, p. 417
683	Georges Cr.				----- Marrah	v. 27q, p. 417
684	Georges Cr.				Wm. Read	v. 27q, p. 417
685	Six Mile Cr.	Jno. Green	500	1798		v. 37, p. 192
686	Six Mile Cr.				----- Anderson	v. 37, p. 192
687	Six Mile Cr.				Jas. Beaty	v. 37, p. 192
688	Six Mile Cr.	Jas. Gillam	100	1784		v. 3q, p. 105
689	Six Mile Cr.	Robt. Grant	640	1785		v. 5q, p. 113
690	Six Mile Cr.	Jas. Beaty	334	1789		v. 24q, p. 9
691	Six Mile Cr.				Jas. Gillison	v. 24q, p. 9
692	Six Mile Cr.				Robt. Anderson	v. 24q, p. 9
693	Six Mile Cr.	Benj. Lawrence	238	1798		v. 37, p. 26
694	Six Mile Cr.				Jas. Gillison	v. 37, p. 26
695	Crow Creek	Simon Con	50	1798		v. 37, p. 68
696	Crow Creek				Jon Con	v. 37, p. 68
697	Crow Creek	Jannet Gourley	190	1798		v. 37, p. 27
698	Crow Creek	Bernard Glenn	640	1784		v. 5q, p. 39
699	Crow Creek	Leonard Farrar	143	1794		v. 31q, p. 483
700	Crow Creek	Robt. Craven	404	1790		v. 25q, p. 101
701	Crow Creek				----- Glenn	v. 25q, p. 101
702	Crow Creek				Wm. Tate	v. 25q, p. 101
703	Crow Creek	Jas. Bradley	474	1795		v. 32, p. 268
704	Crow Creek				----- Patterson	v. 32, p. 268
705	Crow Creek	Wm. Anderson	426	1791		v. 27q, p. 455

No.	Stream	Name	Acre	Date	Bounded By	Reference
706	Crow Creek				John Wood	v. 27q, p. 455
707	Broad Mouth Cr.	Wm. Bell	273	1799		v. 37, p. 205
708	Broad Mouth Cr.	Jas. Clements	119	1798		v. 37, p. 253
709	Broad Mouth Cr.				Jno. Harper	v. 37, p. 253
710	Broad Mouth Cr.				Walter Bell	v. 37, p. 253
711	Broad Mouth Cr.				Culliver Clements	v. 37, p. 253
712	Broad Mouth Cr.	Chas. Clements	1	1799		v. 37, p. 253
713	Broad Mouth Cr.				David Oliphant	v. 37, p. 253
714	Broad Mouth Cr.				Saml. Smith	v. 37, p. 253
715	Broad Mouth Cr.				James Todd	v. 37, p. 253
716	Broad Mouth Cr.				Andw. Williamson	v. 37, p. 253
717	Broad Mouth Cr.	Richard Sadler	230	1784		v. 3q, p. 184
718	Broad Mouth Cr.	Joshua Gotcher	137	1794		v. 31q, p. 433
719	Broad Mouth Cr.				Jos. Brown	v. 31q, p. 433
720	Broad Mouth Cr.				B. Fowler	v. 31q, p. 433
721	Broad Mouth Cr.				Jacob Reed	v. 31q, p. 433
722	Broad Mouth Cr.				Wm. Gotcher	v. 31q, p. 433
723	Broad Mouth Cr.	Jno. Hallum	200	1784		v. 4q, p. 172
724	Broad Mouth Cr.	Wm. Hort	640	1784		v. 5q, p. 158
725	Broad Mouth Cr.				Jas. Brown	v. 5q, p. 158
726	Broad Mouth Cr.	Thos. Garner	398	1792		v. 28q, p. 258
727	Broad Mouth Cr.				Ambrose Nichelson	v. 28q, p. 258
728	Broad Mouth Cr.	Dickison Garrett	350	1792		v. 27q, p. 551
729	Broad Mouth Cr.	Giles Gant	250	1784		v. 5q, p. 305
730	Broad Mouth Cr.	Aaron Broyles	330	1792		v. 28q, p. 207

No.	Location	Name	Acres	Year	Grantee/Other	Reference
731	Broad Mouth Cr.	Wm. Brown	200	1784		v. 3q, p. 18
732	Broad Mouth Cr.				Jos. Brown	v. 3q, p. 18
733	Broad Mouth Cr.	Jos. Brown	200	1784		v. 3q, p. 15
734	Broad Mouth Cr.	Hugh Brown	200	1784		v. 3q, p. 11
735	Broad Mouth Cr.	Nathl. Aldridge	100	1785		v. 13q, p. 78
736	Broad Mouth Cr.				Wm. Reed	v. 13q, p. 78
737	Broad Mouth Cr.	Hugh Harkins	500	1797		v. 36, p. 134
738	Broad Mouth Cr.				Hugh Brown	v. 36, p. 134
739	Broad Mouth Cr.				Saml. Smith	v. 36, p. 134
740	Broad Mouth Cr.				Walter Harkins	v. 36, p. 134
741	Broad Mouth Cr.	Robt. Anderson	200	1784		v. 2q, p. 225
742	Keowee Riv.	Benj. Lawrence	395	1784		v. 1q, p. 271
743	Keowee Riv.	Jno. Martin	270	1785		v. 5q, p. 219
744	Keowee Riv.	Ephriam Mitchell	640	1784		v. 5q, p. 119
745	Keowee Riv.	David Worthington	426	1786		v. 19q, p. 225
746	Keowee Riv.				Saml. Taylor	v. 19q, p. 225
747	Keowee Riv.				Robt. Anderson	v. 19q, p. 225
748	Keowee Riv.	Fields Pewet	127	1786		v. 19q, p. 221
749	Keowee Riv.				Jas. Ingram	v. 19q, p. 221
750	Keowee Riv.				Wm. Hollen	v. 19q, p. 221
751	Keowee Riv.				Jno. Parsons	v. 19q, p. 221
752	Keowee Riv.	Andw. Pickens, Esq.	573	1784		v. 15q, p. 167
753	Keowee Riv.	Jno. Portman	95	1786		v. 3q, p. 247
754	Keowee Riv.	Fredk. Glover	211	1790		v. 25q, p. 50
755	Keowee Riv.	Jno. Hinnington	231	1791		v. 27q, p. 76
756	Keowee Riv.	Rev. Jno. Harris	250	1784		v. 5q, p. 282

No.	Stream	Name	Acre	Date	Bounded By	Reference
757	Keowee Riv.	Jabez Evans	200	1784		v. 5q, p. 265
758	Keowee Riv.	Abrm. Emery	200	1792		v. 28q, p. 218
759	Keowee Riv.	David Gentry	50	1790		v. 25q, p. 270
760	Keowee Riv.	Jas. Gaily	100	1785		v. 3q, p. 227
761	Keowee Riv.	Abrm. Elledge	350	1789		v. 24q, p. 116
762	Keowee Riv.				Jno. Martin	v. 24q, p. 116
763	Keowee Riv.	Isaac Elledge	356	1792		v. 31q, p. 112
764	Keowee Riv.				Jno. Portman	v. 31q, p. 112
765	Keowee Riv.				Jno. Twilly	v. 31q, p. 112
766	Keowee Riv.	Jno. E. Calhoun	500	1798		v. 37, p. 177
767	Keowee Riv.				Jos. Reed	v. 37, p. 177
768	Keowee Riv.				Wm. Calhoun	v. 37, p. 177
769	Keowee Riv.				Jno. Green	v. 37, p. 177
770	Keowee Riv.	Sarah Verner	400	1789		v. 25q, p. 238
771	Keowee Riv.				Jno. Verner	v. 25q, p. 238
772	Keowee Riv.	Maj. Saml. Taylor	400	1784		v. 5q, p. 246
773	Keowee Riv.				Gen. Pickens	v. 5q, p. 246
774	Keowee Riv.	David Sloan	530	1791		v. 28q, p. 61
775	Keowee Riv.				Aquilla Green	v. 28q, p. 61
776	Keowee Riv.				Jno. Martin	v. 28q, p. 61
777	Keowee Riv.	Capt. Geo. Sidle	300	1784		v. 13q, p. 260
778	Keowee Riv.	Richard Roberts	300	1784		v. 13q, p. 257
779	Keowee Riv.	Wm. Ranfrow	271	1787		v. 14q, p. 207
780	Keowee Riv.				Wm. Pickens	v. 14q, p. 207
781	Keowee Riv.	Jean Anderson	300	1784		v. 4q, p. 84

No.	Location	Grantee	Acres	Year		Reference
782	Keowee Riv.	Jno. Clark	640	1784		v. 6q, p. 273
783	KeoweeeRiv.	Capt. Benj. Brown	240	1795		v. 32, p. 451
784	Keowee Riv.				Rev. Jno. Harris	v. 32, p. 451
785	Keowee Riv.	Josiah Burton	434	1791		v. 27q, p. 288
786	Keowee Riv.	Capt. Jesse Baker	300	1784		v. 13q, p. 244
787	Keowee Riv.				Saml. Taylor	v. 13q, p. 244
788	Keowee Riv.	Alex. Bailie	275	1785		v. 5q, p. 12
789	Keowee Riv.	Stephen Barton	119	1796		v. 32q, p. 661
790	Keowee Riv.				Ellis Harlin	v. 32q, p. 661
791	Keowee Riv.				Felix Warley	v. 32q, p. 661
792	Keowee Riv.	Geo. Benson	300	1784		v. 5q, p. 16
793	Keowee Riv.	John Hays	382	1796		v. 36q, p. 15
794	Keowee Riv.				Henry Hays	v. 36q, p. 15
795	Keowee Riv.	John Irby	172	1798		v. 37q, p. 117
796	Keowee Riv.				W. Daniel	v. 37q, p. 117
797	Keowee Riv.				Isham Irby	v. 37q, p. 117
798	Keowee Riv.	James Jett	225	1799		v. 37, p. 219
799	Keowee Riv.				----- Kelly	v. 37, p. 219
800	Keowee Riv.				----- Kennady	v. 37, p. 219
801	Keowee Riv.	Henry Burch	500	1799		v. 37, p. 329
802	Keowee Riv.	Lt. Col. Jno. Grimke	450	1784		v. 13q, p. 237
803	Keowee Riv.	Richard Walter	200	1785		v. 12q, p. 313
804	Keowee Riv.	Thos. Wapers	640	1784		v. 8q, p. 471
805	Lit. Beaver	Saml. Burton	330	1798		v. 37, p. 10
806	Dam of Tugaloo	Isaiah Greer	241	1798		v. 37, p. 97
807	River				Thos. Holden	v. 37, p. 97

No.	Stream	Name	Acre	Date	Bounded By	Reference
808	Lit. Beaver				Major Parsons	v. 37, p. 97
809	Dam of Tugaloo				Jos. Reed	v. 37, p. 97
810	River	Maj. Saml. Wise	400	1784		v. 14q, p. 332
811	"	Reuben Nash	997	1788		v. 23q, p. 351
812	"	Jno. Harden	415	1793		v. 31q, p. 379
813	"				Robt. Smith	v. 31q, p. 379
814	"	Saml. Dane	350	1787		v. 14q, p. 164
815	"	Jno. Eason	200	1784		v. 13q, p. 203
816	"	David Edmunds	200	1784		v. 13q, p. 207
817	Big Beaver Dam	Jacob Milligan	450	1784		v. 14q, p. 300
818	of Tugaloo Riv.	Maj. Andw. Ellient	400	1784		v. 13q, p. 199
819	"	Chas. Haney	374	1797		v. 36, p. 149
820	"				Wm. Sullivan	v. 36, p. 149
821	"				Gabriel Davis	v. 36, p. 149
822	"				Minor Winn	v. 36, p. 149
823	"	Wm. Hickman	320	1799		v. 37, p. 206
824	"				Thos. Farrar	v. 37, p. 206
825	"				Gen. Hughes	v. 37, p. 206
826	"				----- McCambridge	v. 37, p. 206
827	"	Wm. Donnan	300	1784		v. 13, p. 196
828	"	Lt. Jas. Doyley	200	1784		v. 13, p. 198
829	"	Dever. Driggs	200	1784		v. 13q, p. 199
830	"	Jno. Gamball	200	1784		v. 13q, p. 215
831	"	Alex. Gillen	400	1784		v. 13q, p. 204
832	"	Benj. Hickman	348	1794		v. 32, p. 249
833	"				Henry Lowry	v. 32, p. 249

No.	Location	Name	Acres	Year	Second Name	Reference
834	Big Beaver Dam	Geo. Jeffers	200	1784		v. 15q, p. 85
835	of Tugaloo Riv.	Eliz. Miller	620	1789		v. 24q, p. 185
835	"	Chas. Miles	300	1785		v. 17q, p. 105
837	"				Jno. Francis Gorget	v. 17q, p. 105
838	"	Danl. Keith	300	1785		v. 11q, p. 306
839	"				Alex. Keith	v. 11q, p. 306
840	"	Jas. Rutherford	300	1792		v. 28q, p. 285
841	"	Jno. Begly	200	1784		v. 15q, p. 69
842	"	Lt. Chas. Brown	200	1784		v. 15q, p. 66
843	"	Geo. Blackmore	200	1784		v. 15q, p. 75
844	"	Col. R. Anderson	200	1785		v. 7q, p. 141
845	"	Wm. Grant	244	1801		v. 38, p. 499
846	"	Jas. Shirley	300	1784		v. 3q, p. 175
847	"	Robt. Spence	110	1785		v. 14q, p. 284
848	"				Saml. Dylrumple	v. 14q, p. 284
849	"				Wm. Miller	v. 14q, p. 284
850	"	Hugh Wardlaw	427	1785		v. 8q, p. 470
851	Big Beaver Dam	Jno. Abney	300	1786		v. 21q, p. 130
852	of Rocky Riv.				Wm. Turner	v. 21q, p. 130
853	"				----- Bartlet	v. 21q, p. 130
854	"				Jonathan Gilbert	v. 21q, p. 130
855	"				Polly Taylor	v. 21q, p. 130
856	"				Peter Gottoway	v. 21q, p. 130
857	"				Thos. Hampton	v. 21q, p. 130
858	"	Col. Robert Anderson	200	1785		v. 7q, p. 141
859	"				Andw. Ross	v. 7q, p. 141

No.	Stream	Name	Acre	Date	Bounded By	Reference
860	Big Beaver Dam				Alex. Moore	v. 7q, p. 141
861	of Ricky Riv.	Saml. Atkins	486	1785		v. 9q, p. 449
862	"				Jas. Miller	v. 9q, p. 449
863	"				Wm. Neils	v. 9q, p. 449
864	"				Jno. Page	v. 9q, p. 449
865	"	Barny Burns	390	1784		v. 1q, p. 45
866	"				Jno. Dugle	v. 1q, p. 45
867	"				Robt. Stewart	v. 1q, p. 45
868	"				Saml. Brown	v. 1q, p. 45
869	"	Thos. Brown	174	1789	Widow Riggs	v. 25q, p. 57
870	"				Robt. Johnston	v. 25q, p. 57
870	"				Saml. Nored	v. 25q, p. 57
872	"					v. 25q, p. 57
873	"	Wm. Eales	640	1784		v. 5q, p. 89
874	"				Wm. Huxham	v. 5q, p. 89
875	"	Alex. Davis	315	1795		v. 32, p. 405
876	"				Philip Porter	v. 32, p. 405
877	"				Oliver Charles	v. 32, p. 405
878	"				Absolom Bryant	v. 32, p. 405
879	"	Thos. Entrekin	200	1784		v. 8q, p. 134
880	"	Field Farrar	640	1784		v. 5q, p. 74
881	"				Jacob Mulligan	v. 5q, p. 74
882	"	Wm. Gough	110	1785		v. 11q, p. 329
883	"				Ralph Smith	v. 11q, p. 329
884	"	Jas. Porter	187	1790		v. 25q, p. 313
885	"	David Oliphant	640	1784		v. 9q, p. 39

No.	Location	Grantee	Acres	Year	Grantee	Reference
886	"	Wm. Huxham	640	1784	Jas. Shirley	v. 9q, p. 39
887	"					v. 5q, p. 192
888	"				Wm. Eales	v. 5q, p. 192
889	Lit. Beaver Dam	Wm. Guy	160	1795		v. 33, p. 399
890	of Rocky Riv.				David Coller	v. 33, p. 399
891	"				Richard Monnow	v. 33, p. 399
892	"	Chas. Goodwin	640	1785		v. 5q, p. 100
893	"				Geo. Anderson	v. 5q, p. 100
894	"				Jas. Ross	v. 5q, p. 100
895	"	Jas. Lincoln	1000	1788		v. 22q, p. 340
896	"				Robt. Young	v. 22q, p. 340
897	"				Alex. McDowall	v. 22q, p. 340
898	Rocky Riv.	Jno. Entrekin	185	1793		v. 29q, p. 118
899	Rocky Riv.	Mary Anderson	539	1785		v. 4q, p. 95
900	Rocky Riv.	Kath. Elsinore	258	1785		v. 4q, p. 391
901	Rocky Riv.	John Harris	170	1794		v. 31q, p. 508
902	Rocky Riv.				----- Martin	v. 31q, p. 508
903	Rocky Riv.				Wm. Lesley	v. 31q, p. 508
904	Rocky Riv.				Robt. Dowdle	v. 31q, p. 508
905	Rocky Riv.	Jno. Gillaird	640	1785		v. 5q, p. 123
906	Rocky Riv.	Jno. Pairson	150	1784		v. 10q, p. 539
907	Rocky Riv.	Jno. Irwin	250	1785		v. 13q, p. 17
908	Rocky Riv.				Capt. David Hopkin	v. 13q, p. 17
909	Rocky Riv.	Adam Stuart	200	1784		v. 10q, p. 529
910	Rocky Riv.				Jno. E. Calhoun	v. 10q, p. 529

No.	Stream	Name	Acre	Date	Bounded By	Reference
911	Rocky Riv.				Jno. Patterson	v. 10q, p. 529
912	Rocky Riv.				Thos. Ramsey	v. 10q, p. 529
913	Rocky Riv.	Jno. Cunningham	640	1784		v. 5q, p. 64
914	Rocky Riv.	Jno. Ehney	250	1785		v. 2q, p. 155
915	Rocky Riv.	Wm. Buchannan	250	1785		v. 13q, p. 3
916	Rocky Riv.				Hugh Warnoch	v. 13q, p. 3
917	Rocky Riv.	Jno. Hillhouse	500	1799		v. 37, p. 277
918	Rocky Riv.				John Henry	v. 37, p. 277
919	Rocky Riv.				Alex. McClesky	v. 37, p. 277
920	Rocky Riv.				Saml. Derumple	v. 37, p. 277
921	Rockey Creek	Thos. Garner	457	1799		v. 37, p. 333
922	Rockey Creek				Thos. Carder	v. 37, p. 333
923	Rockey Creek				Hugh Wilson	v. 37, p. 333
924	Rockey Creek				Wm. Hona	v. 37, p. 333
925	Rockey Creek	Wm. Bell	500	1799		v. 37, p. 331
926	Rockey Creek	Benj. Arnold	1000	1793		v. 27q, p. 266
927	Rockey Creek	Reuben Clemons	402	1793		v. 31q, p. 103
928	Rockey Creek				Jas. Clemons	v. 31q, p. 103
929	Rockey Creek				Ambrose Nickles	v. 31q, p. 103
930	Rockey Creek	Jas. Coil	425	1785		v. 6q, p. 96
931	Rockey Creek	Fogus Caven	135	1791		v. 27q, p. 461
932	Rockey Creek				Martha Coil	v. 27q, p. 461
933	Rockey Creek				Jas. Coil	v. 27q, p. 461
934	Rockey Creek				Alex. Erwin	v. 27q, p. 461
935	Rockey Creek	John Ernest	300	1784		v. 14q, p. 307

No.	Location	Name	Acres	Year	Name 2	Reference
936	"				Jno. Huger	v. 14q, p. 307
937	"				Wm. Smith	v. 14q, p. 307
938	"	Jas. Huston	127	1785		v. 8q, p. 311
939	"	Geo. Joorr	101	1799		v. 37, p. 339
940	"				Geo. Dilworth	v. 37, p. 339
941	"				Wm. Harper	v. 37, p. 339
942	"	Wm. Honey	265	1799		v. 37, p. 418
943	"				Jno. Nickelson	v. 37, p. 418
944	"				Wm. Honey, Jr.	v. 37, p. 418
945	"	John Budd	200	1787	Moses Langley	v. 12q, p. 79
946	"					v. 12q, p. 79
947	"	Jno. Duglas	171	1784		v. 1q, p. 223
948	"	Nathan Brient	150	1788		v. 24q, p. 28
949	"				Robt. Young	v. 24q, p. 28
950	"				Moses Tomblen	v. 24q, p. 28
951	Chauga Creek	Jas. Doran	420	1798	Wm. Stephen	v. 37, p. 163
952	Chauga Creek					v. 37, p. 163
953	Chauga Creek	Moses Jones	168	1798		v. 37, p. 37
954	Chauga Creek					v. 37, p. 37
955	Chauga Creek	Mary Doran	282	1799	Jno. Lovelady	v. 37, p. 429
956	Chauga Creek				Geo. Blair	v. 37, p. 429
957	Chauga Creek				----- Maximillian	v. 37, p. 429
958	Chauga Creek	Henry Dobson	115	1798		v. 37, p. 162
959	Chauga Creek				Francis Arnold	v. 37, p. 162
960	Chauga Creek				Chas. Pinckney	v. 37, p. 162
961	Chauga Creek				Jas. Blair	v. 37, p. 162

No.	Stream	Name	Acre	Date	Bounded By	Reference
962	Chauga Creek	John Miller	150	1787		v. 12q, p. 78
963	Chauga Creek	Jas. Robertson	200	1784		v. 12q, p. 267
964	Deep Creek	Robert Green	200	1784		v. 1q, p. 180
965	Deep Creek	Rev. Robt. Hall	300	1784		v. 4q, p. 168
966	Deep Creek				Hugh Reid	v. 4q, p. 168
967	Deep Creek	Jas. Huston	640	1784		v. 4q, p. 157
968	Deep Creek	James Jordon	400	1784		v. 5q, p. 396
969	Hurricane Creek	Micajah Clark	724	1799		v. 37, p. 430
970	Hurricane Creek				Jas. Hambleton	v. 37, p. 430
971	Hurricane Creek				Jonathan Clark	v. 37, p. 430
972	Hurricane Creek				Wm. Oatwell	v. 37, p. 430
973	Hurricane Creek	Micajah Clarke	400	1784		v. 5, p. 165
974	Hurricane Creek	Henry Green	676	1791		v. 27q, p. 391
975	Hurricane Creek				Joseph Smith	v. 27q, p. 391
976	Hurricane Creek				Thos. Cooper	v. 27q, p. 391
977	Hurricane Creek	Abednego Green	142	1791		v. 27, p. 524
978	Hurricane Creek				----- Arnel	v. 27, p. 524
979	Hurricane Creek				Thos. Coker	v. 27, p. 524
980	Hurricane Creek	David Clark	200	1784		v. 4q, p. 317
981	Rices Creek	Jas. Adair & Jas. Curry	286	1792	Wm. Benson	v. 31q, p. 11
982	Rices Creek					v. 31q, p. 11
983	Rices Creek	Philip Prator	662	1791		v. 28q, p. 46
984	Rices Creek	Wm. Binum	1000	1794		v. 32, p. 265
985	Rices Creek				----- Kilgore	v. 32, p. 265

70

No.	Location	Grantee	Acres	Year	Adjacent	Reference
986	Rices Creek				Isaac Miller	v. 32, p. 265
987	Rices Creek				Jos. Duncan	v. 32, p. 265
988	Canoe Creek	Jno. Corrie	446	1792		v. 26q, p. 338
989	Canoe Creek				Alex. White	v. 26q, p. 338
990	Canoe Creek				A.C. Jones	v. 26q, p. 338
991	Canoe Creek	Wm. Gillespy	200	1784		v. 3q, p. 357
992	Saluda Riv.	Moses Hendricks	430	1798		v. 37, p. 14
993	Saluda Riv.				Saml. Martain	v. 37, p. 14
994	Saluda Riv.				Nathl. Clark	v. 37, p. 14
995	Saluda Riv.				Jas. Kilgore	v. 37, p. 14
996	Saluda Riv.				Nicholas Edwards	v. 37, p. 14
997	Saluda Riv.	Benj. Barton	104	1785		v. 7q, p. 321
998	Saluda Riv.	Jas. Beal	159	1787		v. 12q, p. 171
999	Saluda Riv.				Stephen Anderson	v. 12q, p. 171
1000	Saluda Riv.				Peter McCane	v. 12q, p. 171
1001	Saluda Riv.				Wm. Anderson	v. 12q, p. 171
1002	Saluda Riv.				----- Wilson	v. 12q, p. 171
1003	Saluda Riv.	Jas. Allison	140	1785		v. 21q, p. 127
1004	Saluda Riv.				Mr. Cock	v. 21q, p. 127
1005	Saluda Riv.				Capt. Robt. Maxwell	v. 21q, p. 127
1006	Saluda Riv.				----- Wagnon	v. 21q, p. 127
1007	Little River	Thos. Boyd	500	1799		v. 37, p. 242
1008	Little River	Ezekiel Pickens	523	1785		v. 17q, p. 247
1009	Little River				Dr. Jas. Martin	v. 17q, p. 247
1010	Little River	Eleazer Turner	200	1784		v. 14q, p. 324
1011	Little River	Jas. Gilham	500	1798		v. 37, p. 101

No.	Stream	Name	Acre	Date	Bounded By	Reference
1012	Little River		1000	1786	Jno. Morehead	v. 37, p. 101
1013	Little River	Capt. Barnard Elliott	300	1784		v. 1q, p. 348
1014	Little River	Capt. Thos. Gadsden	358	1790		v. 13q, p. 242
1015	Little River	Ezekile Buffington				v. 25q, p. 92
1016	Little River	Jas. Feast	200	1784		v. 13q, p. 234
1017	Little River	Jos. Bailey	200	1787		v. 14q, p. 235
1018	Little River	Elijah Baker	200	1786		v. 9q, p. 380
1019	Little River	Jesse Brown	198	1793		v. 29q, p. 143
1020	Little River	Jacob Holland	56	1799		v. 37, p. 279
1021	Little River				Saml. Armstrong	v. 37, p. 279
1022	Little River				David Robinson	v. 37, p. 279
1023	Little River	Jno. Grissum	128	1793		v. 31q, p. 553
1024	Little River		112	1798	Elijah Brown	v. 31q, p. 553
1025	Golden Creek	Jno. Hamilton				v. 37, p. 120
1026	Golden Creek				----- Rice	v. 37, p. 120
1027	Golden Creek	Jno. Brady	208	1789		v. 24q, p. 14
1028	Golden Creek				Elijah Mayfield	v. 24q, p. 14
1029	Golden Creek				Geo. Miller	v. 24q, p. 14
1030	Golden Creek	Jno. Eubanks	875	1891		v. 27q, p. 439
1031	Golden Creek				Thos. Braday	v. 27q, p. 439
1032	Golden Creek	Jas. Rice	292	1785		v. 15q, p. 99
1033	Big Creek	John Harper	61	1799		v. 37q, p. 223
1034	Big Creek				David Anderson	v. 37q, p. 223
1035	Big Creek				Jas. Watkins	v. 37q, p. 223
1036	Big Creek				Wm. Harper	v. 37q, p. 223

No.	Creek	Name	Name 2	Acres	Year	Name 3	Reference
1037	Big Creek	Wm. Fariss		447	1792	Jacob Earnest	v. 31q, p. 111
1038	Big Creek					J. Moore	v. 31q, p. 111
1039	Big Creek					Jno. Gilliland	v. 31q, p. 111
1040	Big Creek					Isaac Horton	v. 31q, p. 111
1041	Big Creek						v. 31q, p. 111
1042	Mile Creek	James Abbet		806	1793		v. 29q, p. 35
1043	Mile Creek					Duncan Cameron	v. 29q, p. 35
1044	Mile Creek	Daniel Bush		198	1785		v. 2q, p. 117
1045	Mile Creek					----- Light	v. 2q, p. 117
1046	Barkers Creek	Barnard Beekman		320	1784		v. 5q, p. 2
1047	Barkers Creek					Richard Brook	v. 5q, p. 2
1048	Barkers Creek					----- Roberts	v. 5q, p. 2
1049	Barkers Creek	Benj. Aldridge		1500	1784		v. 20q, p. 10
1050	Barkers Creek	Geo. Joor		260	1799		v. 37, p. 338
1051	Barkers Creek					Wm. Reed	v. 37, p. 338
1052	Barkers Creek					Jas. Kennady	v. 37, p. 338
1053	Barkers Creek					Jno. Tumage	v. 37, p. 338
1054	Barkers Creek					David Greer	v. 37, p. 338
1055	Barkers Creek					Giles Grant	v. 37, p. 338
1056	Barkers Creek					Caleb Connaway	v. 37, p. 338
1057	Carricks Creek	Alex. Edens		100	1785		v. 3q, p. 224
1058	Carricks Creek	Geo. Hutson		270	1798		v. 37, p. 35
1059	Peters Creek	Jno. Butt		365	1788		v. 23q, p. 339
1060	Peters Creek					Benj. Clark	v. 23q, p. 339
1061	Peters Creek	Jno. Beekman, Jr.		652	1784		v. 4q, p. 139
1062	Peters Creek					Benj. Rany	v. 4q, p. 139

No.	Stream	Name	Acre	Date	Bounded By	Reference
1063	Devils Fork	Francis Albertia	649	1784		v. 2q, p. 239
1064	Devils Fork	Andw. Cunningham	250	1787		v. 20q, p. 322
1065	Devils Fork	Jno. Richardson	640	1784		v. 5q, p. 269
1066	Devils Fork	Morgan Flood	341	1799		v. 37, p. 311
1067	Devils Fork				Stephen Strange	v. 37, p. 311
1068	Devils Fork				Jos. McMurtrey	v. 37, p. 311
1069	Cedar Creek	Henry Hill	365	1799		v. 37, p. 406
1070	Cedar Creek	Thos. Carpenter	1000	1793		v. 31q, p. 246
1071	Doddeys Creek	Richd. Hood	392	1791		v. 27q, p. 286
1072	Doddeys Creek	Howell Dowdy	200	1784		v. 2q, p. 376
1073	Doddeys Creek	Jno. Kelley	331	1785		v. 12q, p. 331
1074	Broadaway Cr.	James Scott	200	1785		v. 12q, p. 149
1075	Broadaway Cr.	Thos. Clemens	486	1792		v. 28, p. 342
1076	Broadaway Cr.				David Wade	v. 28q, p. 342
1077	Broadaway Cr.				Stephen Bennet	v. 28q, p. 342
1078	Broadaway Cr.	Jas. Graham	300	1785		v. 2q, p. 157
1079	Broadaway Cr.	Thos. Moore	200	1785		v. 12q, p. 340
1080	Broadaway Cr.	Jas. Mullwee	200	1784		v. 8q, p. 151
1081	Broadaway Cr.				Robt. Selfridge	v. 8q, p. 151
1082	Broadaway Cr.				Robt. Slwenston	v. 8q, p. 151
1083	Broadaway Cr.	Daniel Norris	200	1785		v. 14q, p. 302
1084	Broadaway Cr.	Peter Chamblers	200	1785		v. 13q, p. 193
1085	Broadaway Cr.	Jno. Clappard	200	1785		v. 13q, p. 194
1086	Broadaway Cr.				Jno. Peter Ward	v. 13q, p. 194
1087	Cherokee Cr.	Thos. Bonner	150	1784		v. 2q, p. 188

No.	Location	Grantee	Name	Acres	Year	Reference
1088	Cherokee Cr.	Hannah Horton		617	1785	v. 4q, p. 147
1089	Cherokee Cr.	Wm. Lawrence		500	1773	v. 16q, p. 290
1090	Cherokee Cr.		Wm. Blanton			v. 16q, p. 290
1091	Cherokee Cr.		Alex. Mountrie			v. 16q, p. 290
1092	Cherokee Cr.		Capt. Coomber			v. 16q, p. 290
1093	Cherokee Cr.	Christ. Williman		650	1784	v. 6q, p. 150
1094	Cherokee Cr.	Jos. Cart		640	1785	v. 5q, p. 51
1095	Cherokee Cr.		Joshua Turner			v. 5q, p. 51
1096	Cherokee Cr.		Robt. Forsyth			v. 5q, p. 51
1097	Cherokee Cr.		Geo. Reed			v. 5q, p. 51
1098	Cherokee Cr.	Chas. Clements		871	1792	v. 31q, p. 40
1099	Cherokee Cr.		Peter Hall			v. 31q, p. 40
1100	Cherokee Cr.		Saml. Smith			v. 31q, p. 40
1101	Gt. Rocky Cr.	Blake Mauldin		200	1784	v. 5q, p. 351
1102	Gt. Rocky Cr.	Jas. Austin		107	1785	v. 16q, p. 29
1103	Gt. Rocky Cr.	Jas. Barr		200	1784	v. 18q, p. 1
1104	Gt. Rocky Cr.		Wm. Davis			v. 18q, p. 1
1105	Gt. Rocky Cr.	Jos. Culton		440	1784	v. 5q, p. 65
1106	Gt. Rocky Cr.	Jno. Haynie		500	1795	v. 32, p. 354
1107	Gt. Rocky Cr.		Jno. Robison			v. 32, p. 354
1108	Gt. Rocky Cr.		Ann Hanks			v. 32, p. 354
1109	Gt. Rocky Cr.		Wm. Haynie			v. 32, p. 354
1110	Gt. Rocky Cr.	Jas. Ponder		444	1784	v. 17q, p. 349
1111	Gt. Rocky Cr.		Wm. Wood			v. 17q, p. 349
1112	Gt. Rocky Cr.		Andw. Eagen			v. 17q, p. 349
1113	Gt. Rocky Cr.		Jas. Martin			v. 17q, p. 349

No.	Stream	Name	Acre	Date	Bounded By	Reference
1114	Gt. Rocky Cr.	Patrick Norris	300	1784	Jno. Green	v. 17q, p. 349
1115	Gt. Rocky Cr.	Geo. Shoaler	200	1784		v. 15q, p. 266
1116	Gt. Rocky Cr.	Wm. Lessly	200	1784		v. 3q, p. 173
1117	Gt. Rocky Cr.	Francis Gilespie	51	1797		v. 7q, p. 126
1118	Gt. Rocky Cr.					v. 36, p. 103
1119	Gt. Rocky Cr.				Andw. Pickens	v. 36, p. 103
1120	Gt. Rocky Cr.				Mathew Gillaspie	v. 36, p. 103
1121	Noyewee Cr.	Chas. England	129	1798		v. 37, p. 142
1122	Noyewee Cr.				Hugh Brown	v. 37, p. 142
1123	Noyewee Cr.				Edward Box	v. 37, p. 142
1124	Noyewee Cr.	Mordica Fuller	82	1795		v. 27q, p. 357
1125	Mill Creek	Martin Thacker	180	1791		v. 27q, p. 499
1126	Mill Creek	Col. Benj. Cleveland	650	1789		v. 24q, p. 44
1127	Shoal Creek	Wm. Darnall	356	1795		v. 32, p. 508
1128	Shoal Creek				----- Shankling	v. 32, p. 508
1129	Shoal Creek	Jonathan Gregory	143	1788		v. 23q, p. 338
1130	Weavers Creek	Wm. Durram	78	1793		v. 29q, p. 136
1131	Weavers Creek	Moses Hopper	298	1798		v. 37, p. 40
1132	Neils Creek	Jas. Dowdle	77½	1796		v. 32, p. 574
1133	Neils Creek				Elial Moore	v. 32, p. 574
1134	Neils Creek	Spilsby Glenn	195	1790		v. 25q, p. 258
1135	Neils Creek				Geo. Liddle	v. 25q, p. 258
1136	Neils Creek				Robt. Lowdle	v. 25q, p. 258
1137	Kees Creek	Thos. Harbin	100	1798		v. 37, p. 186
1138	Kees Creek				Field Farrow	v. 37, p. 186

No.	Location	Name	Acres	Year	Other	Reference
1139	Kees Creek	Elias Wilburn	250	1788		v. 23q, p. 29
1140	Bucks Creek	John Holland	200	1784		v. 13q, p. 232
1141	Bucks Creek	Robt. Bottle	200	1784		v. 13q, p. 191
1142	Oconey Creek	Benj. Whorton	383	1792		v. 29q, p. 429
1143	Oconey Creek	Wm. Richards	923	1793		v. 33, p. 191
1144	Oconey Creek				Jno. M. Collum	v. 33, p. 191
1145	Pea Creek	Mary Atchinson	640	1784		v. 9q, p. 269
1146	Pea Creek				Danl. Desaussure	v. 9q, p. 269
1147	Pea Creek	Alex. Boyse	320	1785		v. 10q, p. 15
1148	Pea Creek				Hugh Wardlaw	v. 10q, p. 15
1149	Pea Creek	Anna Van Rhyn	640	1784		v. 4q, p. 186
1150	Pea Creek				Robert Pickens	v. 4q, p. 186
1151	Cuffey Creek	Wm. Boyd	350	1787		v. 19q, p. 193
1152	Cuffey Creek				Wm. McCalep	v. 19q, p. 193
1153	Cuffey Creek	Wm. Bobbitt	84	1796		v. 32, p. 528
1154	Cuffey Creek				Robt. Belcher	v. 32, p. 528
1155	Cuffey Creek				Thos. Bacon	v. 32, p. 528
1156	Cuffey Creek				----- Wilson	v. 32, p. 528
1157	Cuffey Creek	Thos. Bacon	40	1791		v. 27q, p. 452
1158	Cuffey Creek				Shadk. Stokes	v. 27q, p. 452
1159	Cuffey Creek	Robt. Boyse	112	1798		v. 37, p. 133
1160	Beaver Creek	Jesse Davis	119	1799		v. 37, p. 235
1161	Beaver Creek				Jno. Jackson	v. 37, p. 235
1162	Beaver Creek	Joshua Benson	1000	1791		v. 27q, p. 408
1163	Beaver Creek				Wm. Lesley	v. 27q, p. 408
1164	Beaver Creek				Jas. Millwee	v. 27q, p. 408

No.	Stream	Name	Acre	Date	Bounded By	Reference
1165	Beaver Creek	Mark Bird	1000	1795	Jos. Culton	v. 27q, p. 408
1166	Beaver Creek					v. 27q, p. 366
1167	Beaver Creek			1797	Jas. Calhoun	v. 27q, p. 366
1168	Beaver Creek	Maria Kays	328			v. 36, p. 78
1169	Beaver Creek				Jno. Mauldin	v. 36, p. 78
1170	Beaver Creek				Jas. Thomson	v. 36, p. 78
1171	Bear Creek	Abigail Davis	100	1785		v. 7q, p. 354
1172	Bear Creek				Jno. Wilkinson	v. 7q, p. 354
1173	Bear Creek				Lt. Jno. Burksland	v. 7q, p. 354
1174	Bear Creek	Saml. Brummitt	370	1786		v. 16q, p. 302
1175	Bear Creek				Henry Wolf	v. 16q, p. 302
1176	Bear Creek	Elijah Brown	259	1792		v. 31q, p. 93
1177	Bear Creek				Jno. Grissum	v. 31q, p. 93
1178	Bear Creek				Wm. Keyton	v. 31q, p. 93
1179	Bear Creek				Stephen Harris	v. 31q, p. 93
1180	Bear Creek	Heirs: Lt. Jno. Bush	200	1785		v. 13q, p. 169
1181	Bear Creek				Edward Dilkenson	v. 13q, p. 169
1182	Bear Creek				Dr. Jos. Hall	v. 13q, p. 169
1183	Bear Creek	Chas. Haynie	154	1798		v. 37, p. 182
1184	Bear Creek				Jno. Hays	v. 37, p. 182
1185	Bear Creek				Wm. Keaton	v. 37, p. 182
1186	Bear Creek				Obidiah Pinkston	v. 37, p. 182
1187	Sugar Creek	Isaac Bogan	300	1784		v. 10q, p. 39
1188	Sugar Creek				Jno. Blasingame	v. 10q, p. 39
1189	Sugar Creek	Jno. Edwards	109	1799		v. 37, p. 401

ID	Location	Name	Acres	Year	Grantee	Reference
1190	Sugar Creek				----- Logan	v. 37, p. 401
1191	Sugar Creek				----- Glen	v. 37, p. 401
1192	Sugar Creek				----- Brown	v. 37, p. 401
1193	Tomassee Riv.	Geo. Askins	200	1784		v. 15q, p. 78
1194	Tomassee Riv.			1784	Wm. Martin	v. 15q, p. 78
1195	Tomassee Riv.	Wm. Merick	200	1784		v. 12q, p. 244
1196	Tomassee Riv.			1784	Bennett Harper	v. 12q, p. 244
1197	Tomassee Riv.	Richard Pollard	300	1784		v. 14q, p. 305
1198	Tomassee Riv.	Elijah Price	200	1784		v. 12q, p. 271
1199	Tomassee Riv.				Bennett Craftor	v. 12q, p. 271
1200	Tomassee Riv.	Jas. Hamilton, Jr.	200	1784		v. 13q, p. 263
1201	Tomassee Riv.				Jno. Hamilton	v. 13q, p. 263
1202	Brushy Creek	Watson Allison	400	1786		v. 11q, p. 146
1203	Brushy Creek				Wm. Allison	v. 11q, p. 146
1204	Brushy Creek				Nimrod Williams	v. 11q, p. 146
1205	Brushy Creek				Saml. Tolbert	v. 11q, p. 146
1206	Brushy Creek				Mrs. Cherry	v. 11q, p. 146
1207	Brushy Creek	Wm. Edmonson	152	1787		v. 21, p. 180
1208	Brushy Creek				----- Rigway	v. 21, p. 180
1209	Brushy Creek	Peter Fayssoux	640	1784		v. 5q, p. 72
1210	Brushy Creek				Rev. Henry Percell	v. 5q, p. 72
1211	Brushy Creek				Theophilus Wyatt	v. 5q, p. 72
1212	Brushy Creek	----- Clayton				
1213	Brushy Creek	Thos. Hallum	200	1784		v. 4q, p. 171
1214	Brushy Creek	Rev. H. Purcell	640	1784		v. 15q, p. 153
1215	Brushy Creek				Thos. C. Russell	v. 15q, p. 153
1216	Brushy Creek	Wm. Riddle	200	1786		v. 14q, p. 279

No.	Stream	Name	Acre	Date	Bounded By	Reference
1217	Brushy Creek				Wm. Allerson	v. 14q, p. 279
1218	Brushy Creek	Saml. Ridgeway	640	1785		v. 6q, p. 236
1219	Brushy Creek	Wm. Emerson	200	1784		v. 3q, p. 92
1220	Brushy Creek	Jno. Cart	640	1785		v. 5q, p. 50
1221	Brushy Creek				Gen. Wm. Moultrie	v. 5q, p. 50
1222	Long Nose Cr.	Jas. Adams	175	1789		v. 24q, p. 1
1223	Perkins Creek	Jos. Dougherty	490	1798		v. 37, p. 55
1224	Perkins Creek				Jno. Hays	v. 37, p. 55
1225	Martins Creek	Alex. Dromgoole	791	1791		v. 27q, p. 270
1226	Martins Creek				----- Martin	v. 27q, p. 270
1227	Martins Creek				Louis D. Martin	v. 27q, p. 270
1228	Martins Creek				----- Miller	v. 27q, p. 270
1229	Martins Creek	Michael Bird	244	1798		v. 37, p. 63
1230	Bartons Creek	Jas. Drummond	192	1798		v. 37, p. 40
1231	Bartons Creek				Lewis Medland	v. 37, p. 40
1232	Lit. Brasstown Cr.	Moses Jones	54	1798		v. 37, p. 36
1233	15 Mile Creek	Bennett Combs	640	1792		v. 28q, p. 77
1234	Gregorys Cr.	Wm. Bush	233	1799		v. 37, p. 209[1]

[1] The references are taken from State Record of Plat Books to be found in the office of the Secretary of State, Columbia, S.C.

C. Residents of 1790

Abbett, James
Abbett, Thomas
Abel, Jerimiah
Acker, Peter
Adams, David
Adams, James
Adams, John
Adams, John, Jr.
Adams, Stephen
Adkins, Hugh
Adkins, William
Aeson, Abraham
Aeson, James
Agin, John
Agnew, James
Airwichs, James
Akins, Ezekiel
Akok, Joshua
Alexander, Asoph
Alexander, Mathew
Allen, Gershon
Allen, James
Allen, Lee
Alred, William
Anderson, Mathew
Anderson, Moses
Anderson, Robert
Anderson, William
Angelee, Alex.
Armstrong, John
Armstrong, Thomas
Armstrong, William
Armstrong, William
Asher, William
Ashlock, James
Askins, George
Austen, Nathan
Baker, John
Baker, Robert
Bannister, William
Banks, John
Barley, Samuel
Barnes, Henry
Barsher, Robert
Bartlett, Nimrod
Barton, Amy
Barton, Benjamin
Barton, Henry
Barton, James
Barton, John
Beard, John
Beavert, John
Beesley, William

Beesly, William
Bell, Jeane
Bennett, Coms
Bennett, Cooper
Bennett, George
Bennett, William
Berry, Enoch
Bettey, James
Betty, John
Betty, William
Biggs, Caleb
Bishop, Isham
Bishop, Nicholas
Bittick, Francis
Black, John
Blair, George
Blair, James
Blair, Mary
Blease, John
Blithe, John
Blithe, Thomas
Boggs, Aaron
Bohannan, William
Bolen, John
Bolen, Joseph
Bolinger, Frederick
Bond, Charles
Boon, Ratliff
Boren, John
Boren, James
Boren, William
Boren, William
Bowen, Robert
Box, Edward
Box, Edward, Sr.
Box, Robert, Jr.
Boyd, Archebald
Boyd, John
Brada, John
Brada, Thomas
Bradcutt, Richard
Bradcutt, Samuel
Bradley, Francis
Bradley, John
Bradley, Lawrence
Bradshaw, Joel
Brandon, Charles
Brasher, Philip
Brian, Absolam
Brian, James
Briant, Aaron
Briant, Hardy
Briant, John
Briant, Nathen

Brice, James
Briles, Joshua
Briner, Benjamin
Briner, Joseph
Brison, Andrew
Brison, Daniel
Brison, James
Brison, John
Brison, Samuel
Brison, William
Brison, William
Brock, Isaac
Brock, Martha
Brooks, George
Brooks, William
Brooksher, James
Brown, Anne
Brown, Benjamin
Brown, David
Brown, David, Jr.
Brown, David, Sr.
Brown, Elijah
Brown, Griffith
Brown, Hugh, Capt.
Brown, James
Brown, James
Brown, John
Brown, John
Brown, John
Brown, Joseph
Brown, Joseph
Brown, Samuel
Brown, Samuel
Brown, Thomas
Brown, William
Brown, William
Bruce, James
Bruce, James
Bruce, William
Bruster, Sheriff
Buckhanan, Thomas
Buffenton, Ezekiel
Bullard, Nethaniel
Burch, Henry
Burchfield, Adam
Burchfield, John
Burdine, Donatha
Burford, Thomas
Burks, Roland
Burks, Samuel
Burney, William
Burns, Alex.
Burns, John
Burris, Edward

Burris, John
Burton, John
Butler, William
Butt, John
Cadden, James
Cairy, Thomas
Calleway, Thomas
Campbell, James
Campbell, Collen
Canada, Joseph
Canada, Joseph
Cane, Jacob
Cane, Snoden
Cannon, Anne
Cannon, James
Cannon, John
Cannon, William
Cantrell, James
Cantrell, Stephen
Capehart, Jacob
Carleton, Joseph
Carley, William
Carpenter, Bosten
Carpenter, William
Carr, David
Carr, James
Carr, Jonathen
Carruthers, John
Carter, David
Case, Thomas
Candel, James
Candel, Thomas
Canendish, Wm. Moore
Chalmbers, Agnes
Chalmbers, Jacob
Chambers, William
Chapman, Joseph
Charles, Oliver
Chastain, James
Chastain, John
Chastain, John
Chastain, Stephen
Childress, John
Chitwood, Daniel
Chitwood, Sharrack
Clardy, Benjamin
Clardy, John
Clark, Benj. Capt.
Clark, George
Clark, Henry
Clark, John Bud
Clark, Johnathan
Clark, Micajah, Capt.
Clarke, William
Clarke, Giddian
Clarke, Joseph

Clarke, Nathaniel
Clarke, Samuel
Clayton, William
Clemmons, Charles
Clemmons, Eleoner
Clebeland, Benj. Esq.
Cleveland, John
Cleveland, William
Cobb, Abiel
Cobb, Asa
Cobb, Henry
Cobb, John
Cochran, James
Coffee, Jesse
Coldwell, David
Collens, Williams
Collett, Sarah
Conneway, Caleb
Copeland, William
Corbin, Peter
Cornelian, Benj.
Corsby, William
Cox, Beverly
Cox, Edward
Cox, James
Cox, George
Cox, Joel
Cox, John
Cox, John
Cox, John
Cox, Reuben
Cox, William
Cox, William
Crage, John
Crane, Samuel
Crane, William
Cravens, Robt., Capt.
Crawford, David
Christilles, John
Crittentown, Jonathen
Crow, Thomas
Crutchfield, Susannah
Crumpton, James
Culton, Joseph
Cummins, Joseph
Cunningham, Elleoner
Cunningham, James
Curtin, David
Davis, Eli
Davis, Isac
Davis, James
Davis, James
Davis, James
Davis, John
Davis, John Lewis
Davis, Joseph

Davis, Lewis
Davis, Margaret
Davis, Surry
Davis, Thomas
Davis, William
Deen, Samuel
Dempsey, William
Denson, William
Denton, Samuel
Derumphle, Samuel
Davenport, James
Dickerson, Eleoner
Dickerson, John
Dickerson, Robert
Dickey, Martha
Dickey, William
Dickson, David
Dickson, John
Dickson, Mathew
Dickson, Michael
Dikes, William
Donnel, Jerimiah
Doss, William
Doss, Claborn
Doss, Jerimiah
Dotson, Nancy
Dotson, Agnes
Dondle, John
Dondle, Robert
Dowen, James
Downen, Josiah
Downing, Joab
Dorothit, James
Drenan, William
Dromgeole, Alex.
Duncan, John
Duncan, Joseph
Duncan, Mack
Duncan, Samuel
Duncan, Thomas
Dunlap, Davis
Dunlap, Jonathan
Dunn, Joseph
Dinnigan, Joseph
Durham, David
Durham, James
Durrow, James
Early, Patrick
Earnest, Jacob, Jr.
Earnest, Jacob, Sr.
Earnist, Aaron
Easley, Robert
Edens, Alex.
Edens, James
Edens, James
Edmundson, William

Edmunson, Caleb
Edwards, Nichalas
Edwards, Thomas
Elledge, Abraham
Elledge, John
Elledge, Isaac
Elledge, Joseph
Elledge, William
Elliott, Thomas
Ellison, James
Ellison, James
Ellison, William
Erwin, Alexander
Erwin, John
Erwin, Rebekah
Erwin, Joseph
Estes, Moses
Evans, George
Evans, John
Evans, John
Evans, Owen
Evans, Robert
Fagan, Moses
Fagan, Philip
Fair, Barney
Faires, James
Faires, William
Fane, Ebenezer
Fane, Reuben
Farmer, Benjamin
Farmer, Benjamin
Farmor, Francis
Farrar, Francis
Farrar, Eleonor
Farrar, Richard
Farrar, Seth
Farrar, Thomas
Herrel, Felton
Fields, Thomas
Files, Adams
Files, James
Files, Jeremiah
Files, John
Files, Mary
Findley, John
Finley, John
Finley, Mary
Findley, John
Finley, John
Finley, Samuel
Finley, Thomas
Fitsjerrel, Ambrose
Flemming, James
Floyd, William
Forbush, William
Forgason, Thomas
Foster, James
Foster, Thomas
Fowler, William

Franklin, Isham
Franklin, Precilla
Franklin, Thomas
Freeman, Amos
French, Simon
French, William
Fuller, Mordica
Fuller, Stephen
Fulshier, Francis
Fulton, Gershom
Gabrial, John
Galleway, William
Gamblin, Joshua
Gambrel, John
Garlin, Elisha
Garlin, Jesse
Garner, Enoch
Garner, James
Garner, Sturdy
Garner, Thomas
Garrett, Dickerson
Garrison, Paul
Garvin, Thomas
Gentry, David
Gerod, Ansel
Gibbs, Johnathon
Gibson, James
Gibson, William
Gilasby, William
Gilaspy, James
Gilaspy, Jimes
Gilaspy, John
Gilaspy, William
Gilaspy, William, Jr.
Gilaspy, William, Sr.
Gillelin, John
Gilleson, Archebald
Gillelin, Jacob
Gillilia, James
Gillilin, John
Gillison, James
Gillum, William
Gibson, Humphry
Gibson, Julius
Glascock, Madden
Glascow, William
Glen, John
Glen, John
Glen, Robert
Glen, Samuel
Gocher, Henry
Gocher, John
Gocher, Joshua
Gocher, William
Golden, Susannah
Goodwinn, Jesse

Goodwinn, Robert
Gorman, Thomas
Goss, Thomas
Graham, Edward
Graham, Edward
Graham, James
Graham, Peter
Grant, William
Gray, David
Gray, Jesse
Gray, Robert
Gray, Thomas
Gray, William
Green, Ebednego
Green, Henry
Green, John
Green, Masheek
Green, Thomas
Green, William
Greenleas, Peter
Greer, James
Greer, John
Greer, Solomon
Gregory, Isaac
Griffen, John
Griffen, William
Grigary, Jonathen
Grimbal, John
Grindel, John, Sr.
Gisham, John
Grisham, John
Guest, Benjamin
Guest, David
Guest, John
Guest, William
Guest, Moses
Guest, William, Sr.
Gunter, William
Holbert, Joel
Holcomb, Joel
Holcomb, John
Holcomb, Zachariah
Hall, Fenton
Hall, Jesse
Hall, John
Hall, Jonathan
Hall, Nathaniel
Hall, Richard
Hall, Robert
Hall, William
Hallum, John
Haltum, Elizabeth
Hamby, Isaac
Hamby, William
Hamilton, Adley
Hamilton, Andrew

Hamilton, David	Hendricks, James	Huse, Charles
Hamilton, James	Hendricks, John	Husten, Samuel
Hamilton, James	Hendricks, Tobias	Husten, Thomas
Hamilton, James	Henley, Peter	Hutchens, Michael
Hamilton, James, Capt.	Henry, Samuel	Hutson, George
Hamilton, John	Henson, James	Hutson, John
Hamilton, John	Henson, Joseph	Ingle, Paul
Hamilton, John	Henson, Samuel	Ingram, Shadrock
Hamilton, Nenian	Henson, William	Ingram, William
Hamilton, Thomas	Herren, Jacob	Irby, Isham
Hamilton, William	Herrin, Stephen	Isaacs, Elizah
Hamilton, William	Herrin, William	Isaacs, Richard
Hammons, William	Hickman, Benjamin	Isaacs, Samuel
Haney, Charles	Hill, David	Isbell, Gorfrey
Haney, William	Hill, Jonas	Isball, Pendleton
Hanks, Ann	Hill, Mary	Istell, Pendleton
Hardin, Gabriel	Hill, Thomas	Ivy, John
Hardin, John	Hill, William	Ivy, Lott
Hardin, Joseph	Hobbs, William	Jack, James
Hargreaves, Christ	Hodge, Martha	Jackson, Ephraim
Harkins, Hugh	Hodge, William	Jackson, John
Hartness, Robert	Hogg, Giddian	Jackson, Samuel
Harling, Ellis	Holcomb, Hermin	Jackson, William
Harper, Bannister	Holden, Richard	James, Aaron
Harper, John	Holland, James	Jay, Aeson
Harper, Samuel	Holland, Moses	Jeanway, Joseph
Harper, William	Holland, Thomas	Jemison, William
Harris, Benjamin	Holly, John	Jepares, Robert
Harris, Charles	Hohns, James	Jerden, James
Harris, John	Honey, Abner	Jett, James
Harris, John	Honey, William	Jewill, William
Harris, John	Hodd, John	Johnson, Jacob
Harris, Stephen	Hodd, Morgan	Johnson, John
Harris, Japhaniah	Hodd, Richard	Johnson, Michael
Harrison, Barzilla	Hodd, Thomas	Johnson, Noblett
Harrison, Burr	Hooper, Andrew	Johnson, Reuben
Harrison, Thomas	Hooper, Elizabeth	Johnson, Nelson
Haynie, John	Hooper, Mathew	Jolly, James
Haynie, Stephen	Hopkins, John	Jolly, William
Hays, George	Hopper, Moses	Jones, Anne
Hays, Henry	Hornaday, John	Jones, Daniel
Hays, John	Horton, Henry	Jones, Elizabeth
Hays, John	Huggans, John	Jones, James
Hays, Thomas	Huggans, Robert	Jones, John
Hays, Thomas	Huggans, William	Jones, Lewis
Hays, William	Hulet, Martin	Jones, Moses
Heath, William	Hull, Joseph	James, Peter
Hencock, Joseph, Jr.	Hunnicut, Hartwell	Jones, Samuel
Hemroe, David	Hunnicut, John	Jones, Thomas
Hencock, Joseph, Sr.	Hunnicut, Randol	Jones, Willis
Henderson, Robert	Hunt, Charles	Lavan, Alexander
Henderson, Thomas	Hunt, William	Kees, Elijah
Henderson, Thomas	Hunter, John	Kees, Jacob
Henderson, William	Huntsucker, Nichalos	Kees, John, Capt.
Henderson, William	Huse, Andrew	Keetan, William
		Kell, James

Kell, John
Kelley, John
Kelly, John
Kemip, Edward
Kemp, Hardin
Kempton, James
Kerby, David
Kersey, Christ
Kersey, Isaac
Kevan, Forgus
Kieth, Alexander
Kilburn, Henry
Kilgore, Charles
Killen, William
Kilpatrick, Alexander
Kilton, David
King, John
King, Robert, Jr.
King, Robert, Sr.
Kinsey, Peter
Kittle, Jacob
Kiker, Thomas
Lad, Amos
Laderdale, John
Lafoon, William
Laman, Robert
Lambert, David
Lancaster, Richard
Land, John
Land, Joseph, Jr.
Land, Joseph, Sr.
Land, Lewis
Land, William
Land, William
Landers, John
Langley, Joseph
Lankford, Eli
Lasey, James
Lasey, William H.
Latta, David
Lawrence, Benjamin
Lay, Charles
Lee, Joshua
Lee, William
Lennard, Robert
Lennard, Thomas
Lesley, Thomas
Lesley, William
Lethetter, Mimreford
Lewallen, Joseph
Lewis, William
Lewny, Robert
Liddle, Moses
Luice, Henry
Luice, John
Luice, Peter

Luice, Samuel
Linch, Isaac
Lindley, William
Linn, James
Linn, Priseiller
Lindsay, James
Little, Jonah
Little, William
Loften, Samuel
Loften, Thomas
Logan, James
Logan, Joseph
Loggans, James
Lohlan, Anthony
Lohlan, James
Loller, Jacob
Long, Chris
Long, James
Long, John Reed
Looper, Joseph
Loosk, Henry
Loosk, Nathen
Lowe, Easle
Lowe, William
Lowry, Henry
Loyd, Charles
Loyd, John
Loyd, William
Lyons, John
McChesney, Walter
McClokey, Samuel
McCloskey, Joseph
McClure, James
McCollak, (Widow)
McCollister, Alex.
McCrary, Robert
McCurdy, Rhoda
McDonald, James
McFarshen, William
McGill, Samuel
McGriffin, William
McKesley, Moses
McKesley, William
McKesley, Samuel
McKey, William
McKinney, James
McKinsey, Duncan
McKinsey, John
McKoy, Daniel
McKutchen, John
McLain, Alex.
McLain, David
McLaskey, William
McCrary, Alexander
McCollum, Daniel
McCollum, Samuel

McMahan, John
McMahan, Peter
McMahan, Robert
McMahan, William
McMillion, Daniel
McOllister, Francis
McOllister, Nathen
McVay, John
McVay, Margaret
McWilliams, Andrew
McWilliams, James
McWilliams, Williams
Mafield, Ambrose
Mafield, Isham
Mafield, John
Mafield, Stephen
Mahon, Alexander
Manson, William
Maples, John
Marchbanks, William
Martin, Eleoner
Martin, George
Martin, Giddian
Martin, John
Martin, Joseph
Martin, Lewis, D.
Martin, Samuel
Martin, Valentine
Martin, William
Mason, Ezekiel
Mason, Richard
Mason, Richard
Mattison, James
Mauldin, Joab
Mauldin, John
Maxwell, Elisha
Maxwell, John
Means, William
Meeks, Littleton
Mehehah, Ferrel
Melawn, Jonathan
Middleton, John
Miles, John
Miller, Francis
Miller, John
Miller, John, Esq.
Miller, Robert
Milwee, James
Miree, Henry
Miskelley, William
Moor, Aaron
Moore, Burt
Moore, Eliab
Moore, Hugh
Moore, John
Moore, Jonathen

Moore, Robert	Otwell, William	Prater, Phillip
Moore, William	Owen, James	Prestage, Joshua
Morgan, Charles	Owen, Ralph	Pretchard, William
Morgan, Mathew	Owen, William	Price, Joseph
Morgan, Stephen	Owenby, Arther	Price, Kellum
Morris, John	Pannel, Evans	Prince, Richard
Morris, Richard	Park, John	Putman, Barnet
Morrow, John	Parks, William	Putman, Daniel
Morrow, Thomas	Parks, William	Putman, Thomas
Moss, Elizabeth	Parsons, James	Putteet, Tobias
Moss, Jeffs	Parsons, Thomas	Rucane, John
Moss, Thomas	Parsons, William	Roper, Thomas
Mulkey, Phillip	Patterson, James	Reed, Jacob
Munjoy, Jordan	Patterson, John	Reed, James
Murdick, David	Peayne, Moses	Reed, Joseph
Murphey, David	Pepper, John	Reed, Millicent
Murphey, James	Perkins, Isaac	Reed, Nathaniel
Murphy, John	Perkins, John	Reed, Richard
Murphey, Levi	Perkins, Joseph	Reed, William
Murphey, Moses	Perkins, Moses	Reeves, Burgess
Murphey, Solomon	Perkins, Solomon	Reeves, George
Murphey, William	Perkins, Stephens	Reeves, John
Murray, Johnson	Perkins, Ute	Reeves, Jorden
Murray, William	Perkins, William, Capt.	Reeves, Timothy
Murrey, James	Perry, Nathaniel	Renfrow, William
Murrey, William	Pew, David	Rhame, Jacob
Musteen, William	Pew, Willeby	Rice, Charles
Nail, Archibald	Pew, William	Rice, Ezekiel
Nalley, Abraham	Pewett, Drury	Rice, James
Nash, James	Pewett, Field	Richardson, Mathias
Nation, Joseph	Pewett, Thomas	Richardson, Richard
Neale, Samuel	Picclesimore, Henry	Riddle, Andrew
Nelson, Edward	Pickens, Andrew, Esq.	Rider, Christ
Nelson, George	Pickens, Eleoner	Ridera, James
Nelson, William	Pickens, Isreal	Ridesdale, John
Neville, William	Pickens, Robert	Riggs, Elizabeth
Nichols, Ambrose	Pierce, Levi	Right, Adam
Nicholason, John, Capt	Pile, Nicolas	Roach, Elizabeth
Nicholson, William	Pile, William	Robertson, Sarah
Norton, Edward	Pilgrim, Ezekiel	Roberts, Amos
Nunn, Frances	Pilgrim, William	Roberts, Elias
Obar, Daniel	Pitman, Samuel, Jr.	Roberts, Isaac
Obar, Robert	Pitman, Samuel, Sr.	Roberts, James
Odier, Elizabeth	Pitts, Mark	Roberts, John
Oldham, George	Porter, Phillip	Roberts, William
Oldham, James	Porter, Samuel	Roberts, Zachariah
Oldham, Richard	Portman, John	Roberts, Zephemiah
Oliver, Benjamin	Potter, Thomas	Robertson, John
Oliver, Elijah	Powel, Richard	Robertson, Mary
Oliver, Elizabeth	Powel, Robert	Robertson, Nethaniel
Oliver, James	Power, Alexander	Robertson, Richard
Oliver, John	Power, William	Robertson, Samuel
Ore, Alexander	Prater, Archeles	Robertson, Samuel
Osburn, Thomas	Prater, John	Robertson, Thomas
Osburn, William	Pewett, David	Roe, Andrew

Roe, John
Roe, Solomon
Rogers, Hugh
Rogers, Mary
Roland, Charles
Roland, Peter
Rolston, Lewis
Roper, John
Rose, Samuel
Rose, William
Ross, John
Rottan, John
Rush, Jesse
Russel, Edmund
Russel, George
Russel, John
Sadler, George
Sailors, John
Sanders, Henry
Saterfield, James
Saterfield, Jesse
Saterfield, Robert
Saterfield, William
Sawyers, Robert
Saxon, Robert
Saxon, Robert, Jr.
Saxon, Robert, Sr.
Scot, James
Scot, John
Seright, William
Serimsher, Robert
Shannon, John
Shelton, Lewis
Shered, Alexander
Sherewood, Holand
Sherrel, Lewis
Shields, James
Shields, William
Shockley, James
Shockley, Thomas
Shirler, George
Siler, Wilmore
Silman, Benjamin
Simpson, Hugh
Simpson, John, Capt.
Simpson, Hugh
Simpson, Reuben
Simpson, William
Sincler, Alex.
Sincler, Robert
Jacob, Skelton
Jacob, Robert
Jacob, William
Slatten, George
Sloan, David

Sloan, William
Smelcer, George
Smith, Abraham
Smith, Benjamin
SMith, Daniel
Smith, David
Smith, Edwin
Smith, Eleaser
Smith, George
Smith, Henry
Smith, Job
Smith, John
Smith, Stephen
Smith, Joseph
Smith, Mary
Smith, Rachel
Smith, Robert
Smith, Samuel
Smithson, Marsin
Solomon, King
Spencer, Moses
Standage, James
Standage, Thomas
Stanley, William
Stanton, William
Starart, Benjamin
Starart, James
Starns, Frederick
Starns, Margaret
Steel, Isaac
Steel, Vilot
Steel, William
Step, John
Step, Joseph
Stephens, Benjamin
Stephens, David
Stephens, Masheck
Stephens, Thomas
Stephenson, Alex.
Stephenson, David
Stephenson, John
Stephenson, James
Stephenson, Robert
Stephenson, William
Stephinson, James
Stewart, William
Stone, Solomon
Stone, William
Stringer, Daniel
Strange, Stephen
Stripling, William
Swan, James
Tallant, John
Tansey, Abraham
Tansey, William

Tarrictor, John
Tate, James
Taylor, Joanna
Taylor, John
Taylor, Samuel
Telford, Robert
Tennison, John
Terrel, Moses
Terril, Aaron
Thacker, Elizabeth
Thacker, Nathan
Thacker, Ransom
Thacker, Thomas
Thommas, Alex.
Thommas, Evard
Thommas, John
Thompson, George
Thompson, James
Thompson, Mathew
Thompson, Robert
Thompson, William
Thornton, David
Thrasher, Isaac
Timms, Vinson
Tinsley, John
Tippin, John
Titsworth, Isaac
Tood, Jeane
Tommhill, Andrew
Tomhill, Ealenor
Torory, John
Tourlellet, Easa
Tripp, William
Tucker, George
Tucker, Harbert
Turner, Benjamin
Turner, Elizabeth
Turner, John
Turner, Mathias
Turner, Nathen, Jr.
Turner, Nathen, Sr.
Turner, Thomas
Twitty, William
Vance, Jacob
Vandergrift, Garrett
Vandergrift, Leonard
Vanderpool, Abraham
Vanderpool, Winant
Vann, William
Vaughn, James
Vaughn, Joel
Veech, Elijah
Vency, Robert
Vernon, David
Vernon, John

Visage, John	Whorton, Benjamin
Wade, David	Whorton, Isaac
Wade, Edward	Wiatt, William
Wafer, Francis	Wiley, John
Wafer, Thomas	Wilkinson, John
Wagmon, Peter	Wilkinson, Michael
Wakefield, John	Willbanks, Henry
Wakefield, William	Williams, Alex.
Walker, Charles	Williams, Caleb
Walker, Samuel	Williams, Daniel
Walker, Vann	Williams, Edmond
Walker, Zachariah	Williams, Harden
Walles, Richard	Williams, Edward
Walter, Margaret	Williams, Nathaniel
Ward, John	Williams, Price
Ward, Samuel	Willis, Stephen
Ward, Sarah	Willson, John
Ward, Thomas	Wilson, Andrew
Ware, Edward	Wilson, James
Warnook, Joseph	Wilson, John
Warren, William	Wilson, John, Capt.
Wasden, Mary	Wilson, Mary
Washington, William	Wilson, Sarrett
Waters, Charles	Wilson, Thomas
Waters, Philemon	Wilson, William
Watherspoon, David	Wimms, George
Watson, Jonathen	Wimpey, David
Watt, James	Winchester, Daniel
Weaver, John	Wofford, Absolem
Weaver, Samuel	Wollem, Bartholomew
Welborn, Aaron	Womack, Jacob
Welborn, James	Wood, Brazeal
Welch, David	Wood, Jesse
Welch, William	Wood, Samuel
West, Jacob	Woodal, John
Wheeler, Ambrose	Woodal, Joseph
Wheeler, James	Woodside, John
Wheeler, John	Wooten, John
Wheeler, William	Wooten, Frederick
Whilkil, Francis	Wooten, William
Whilkil, William	Wornock, Andrew
White, Alexander	Wright, Moses
White, Alex., Jr.	Young, Andrew
White, Bartholomew	Young, Barbara
White, Benjamin	Young, Ezekiel
White, Charles	Young, John
White, Patrick	Young, Joshua
White, Solomon	Young, Nathen 1
White, Thomas	Young, William
White, William	
Whiteside, Francis	
Whitmex, Joseph	
Whitmire, Michael, Jr.	
Whitmire, Michael, Sr.	
Whitmire, Stephen	
Whitney, John	

1 Heads of Families, op. cit., South Carolina

88

IV. Bibliography.

Source Material

Manuscripts:

South Carolina State Archives. Office of the Historical Commission of South Carolina, Columbia, S.C.

Council Journals

Journals of the Commons House of Assembly

Meyer, A.H., of Clemson College, South Carolina. A letter pertaining to the Soils of Pickens County, South Carolina. (In the possession of the Writer.)

State Record of Land Plats, vols. 1 to 38 inclusive. To be found in the office of the Secretary of State, Columbia, South Carolina.

Printed Sources:

Cooper, Thomas, The Statutes at Large of South Carolina, vols. First through Seventh. Printed by A.S. Johnston, Columbia, South Carolina, 1836 to 1840.

McLendon, W.E., United States Department of Agriculture, Bureau of Soils, Milton Whitney, Chief. Issued October 12, 1910. Soil Survey of Anderson County, South Carolina. Washington: Government Printing Office, 1910.

McLendon, W.E., and Latimer, W.J., United States Department of Agriculture, Bureau of Soils, Milton Whitney, Chief, Issued December 16, 1908. Soil Survey of Oconee County, South Carolina. Washington: Government Printing Office, 1908.

North, S.N.D., Director, Department of Commerce and Labor, Bureau of the Census, Heads of Families at the First Census of the United States in the year 1790, South Carolina, North Carolina, Virginia, Maryland, and Pennsylvania, Washington: Government Printing Office, 1917.

Revolutionary Records of the State of Georgia, vol. 1, Compiled by Allen D. Candler, Atlanta, Georgia, The Franklin-Turner Company. Printers-Publishers-Binders, 1908.

Salley, A.S. Jr., Bulletins of the Historical Commission of South Carolina, No. 4. George Hunter's Map of the Cherokee Country and the Path thereto in 1780, The State Company, Columbia, South Carolina. 1917.

Watson, E.J., Commissioner, Handbook of South Carolina, Second Edition, 1908. The State Department of Agriculture, Commerce, and Immigration. The State Company, Columbia, South Carolina, 1908.

Secondary Material.

Bartram, William, The Travels, Macy-Masius: Publishers, 1828.

Chapman, John, History of South Carolina, Everett Waddy Company, Publishers and Printers, Richmond, Virginia, 1895.

Crane, Verner C., The Southern Frontier, 1670-1732, Durham, North Carolina, Duke University Press, 1928.

Drayton, John, Memoirs of the American Revolution from its Commencement to the Year 1776, inclusive; as relating to the State of South Carolina, vols. 1-11. Printed by A.E. Miller, 120 Broad Street, Charleston, South Carolina, 1821.

Howe, George, A History of the Upper Country of South Carolina, vol. 1. Published by S.C. Courtenay and Company, Charleston: P.B. Glass. Columbia, S.C. 1859.

Mills, Robert, Statistics of South Carolina, Charleston, South Carolina. Hurlbut and Lloyd. 1826.

McCrady, Edward, The History of South Carolina Under the Royal Government, New York: The Macmillan Company.

McCrady, Edward, The History of South Carolina in the Revolution 1775-1780. New York: The Macmillan Company; London: Macmillan and Company, Ltd. 1901.

Ramsay, David, History of South Carolina, Published and sold by W.J. Duffie, Newberry, South Carolina. Printed by Walker, Evans and Company, Charleston S.C. 1858.

INDEX

Calhoun, Jno. Ewing 55
Calhoun, Jno. 53
Calhoun, Jno. E. 62, 67
Calhoun, John 24, 36
Calhoun, Patrick 16
Calhoun, Patrick Ensign 9
Calhoun, Wm. 62
Calhouns 6
Call, Benj. 53
Callahan, Jno. 58
Callahan, Joel 58
Calvert, Jno. 57
Calvert, John 22
Cambridge, Tobias 36
Cameron 17
Cameron, Alexander 8, 9
Cameron, Duncan 73
Cammeron, Duncan 55
Camp, Bradford 55
Camp, Edward 35
Campbell, Archibald 35
Campbell, Daniel 33
Cannon, Jas. 35, 37
Cannon, Jno. 56
Cannon, John 35
Capehart, Jacob 21, 35
Carder, Thos. 68
Carew, Jno. 57
Carpenter, Thomas 23
Carpenter, Thos. 74
Carpenter, Ulrig 54
Cart, Jno. 80
Cart, Jos. 75
Carter, Jesse 40
Caruther, Jno. 54
Case, Jos. 50
Case, Joseph 38
Casedy, Maurica 55
Caven, Fogus 68
Chambers, Peter 30
Chamblers, Peter 74
Chapman, Saml. 52
Cahpman, Samuel 22
Charles, Oliver 66
Chastain, Edw. 42
Chavees, Jno. 48
Chavees, John 30
Cherry, Mrs. 79
Chiles, Henry 55
Clappard, Jno. 74
Clappard, John 30
Clark, Benj. 42, 73
Clark, Bowling 52
Clark, David 70
Clark, Gideon 30, 32, 48
Clark, James 49
Clark, Jno. 63, 70
Clark, Jonothan 52, 70
Clark, Micajah 21, 23, 49, 70
Clark, Nathl. 71
Clark, William 24
Clark, Wm. 48

Clayton 79
Clearman, Jacob 41
Clemens, Thos. 74
Clements, Charles 23
Clements, Chas. 60, 75
Clements, Culliver 60
Clements, James 23
Clements, Jas. 60
Clemons, Jas. 68
Clemons, Reuben 68
Cleveland, Benj. 49, 76
Cleveland, Jno. 48
Cleveland, Larkin 48
Cleveland, Wm. 48
Cobb, Humphrey 32
Cobb, Humphry 22
Cobb, Samuel 41
Cock, Mr. 71
Coil, Jas. 68
Coil, Martha 68
Coker, Thos. 70
Coller, David 67
Collum, Jno. M. 77
Combs, Bennett 23, 80
Con, Jon 59
Con, Simon 59
Connaway, Caleb 73
Coomber 75
Cooper, Thos. 70
Coram, Robt. 35
Cordridge, James 5
Corrie, Jno. 71
Corrie, John 23
Courtney, James 22, 41
Cox, John 36
Cox, Thos. 49
Coytomore, Ensign 6
Craftor, Bennett 79
Craig, John 22, 36
Craswell, Geo. 56
Craswell, Jas. 36
Craven, Robt. 59
Crawford, James 21
Crawford, Jas. 48
Creswell, Mary 42
Cross, Daniel 46
Crowley, Chas. 34
Cuhen 38, 50
Culton, Jos. 75
Culton, Jos. 78
Cunningham 40
Cunningham, Andw. 74
Cunningham, Jno. 68
Cunningham, Patrick 7
Cunningham, Robert 7
Currell, Jno. 43
Currell, John 30
Curry, James 22, 40 70
Curtis, Chichester 36
Dalrymple, Saml. 47, 65
Dane, Saml. 64
Daniel, W. 63

Darnall, William 23
Darnall, Wm. 76
Davey, John 33
Davidson, Thos. 51
Davis, Abigail 78
Davis, Alex. 66
Davis, Alexander 23
Davis, Ambrose 5
Davis, Eli 21, 56
Davis, Gabriel 64
Davis, Harmin 30, 55
Davis, Isaac 42
Davis, James 42
Davis, Jas. 42
Davis, Jesse 77
Davis, Lewis 55
Davis, Wm. 75
Dean, Anthony 5
Dedley, Ambrose 43
Denton, Reuben 30, 49
Derumple, Saml. 68
Desaussure, Danl. 77
Deyer 49
Dickenson, Michael 35
Dickey, James 22, 45
Dickison, Michael 36
Dickson, Saml. H. 50, 51
Dickson, Samuel 24
Dickson, Samuel H. 23
Dickson, Samuel Henry 43
Dickson, Walter C. 35, 38
Dickson, Wm. 56
Dikison, 35
Dilkenson, Edward 78
Dilworth, Geo. 69
Dinkins, Lewis 57
Divenport, Jas. 41
Dobbins, Starret 35
Dobson, Henry 21, 52, 69
Donnam, William 30
Donnan, Wm. 64
Donoon, David 36
Doran, Jas. 69
Doran, Mary 69
Dougherty, Cornelius 4
Dougherty, Jos. 80
Dougherty, Joseph 24
Dowdle, Jas. 76
Dowdle, Robert 67
Dowdy, Howell 74
Downes, Major 9
Downing, John 5
Doyle, Simeon 38
Doyley, James 30
Doyley, Jas. 64
Dranan, Thos. 46
Drayton, Jacob 45
Drayton, William Henry 3
Drennan, John 51
Driggs, Dever. 64
Driggs, Devereaux 30
Dromgoole, Alex. 80
Dromgoole, Alexander 21

Drummond, James 23
Drummond, Jas. 80
Duglas, Jno. 69
Dugle, Jno. 66
Dunbar, Thomas 30
Dunbar, Thos. 51
Duncan, Jos. 53, 54, 57, 71
Duncan, Joseph 21
Durley, Arthur 23, 46
Durley, Jno. 46
Durram, William 23
Durram, Wm. 76
Dutilly, James 51
Dyer, Joshua 24, 50
Dylrumple, Saml. 65
Dyole, Simeon 50
Eagen, Andw. 75
Eales, Wm. 66, 67
Earle, Baylis 49
Earle, Elias 49
Earle, Saml. 54
Earnest, Jacob 73
Easley, Robt. 57
Eason, Jno. 64
Eason, John 30
East, Josiah 46
Easton, Wm. 36
Eckols, Joshua 23, 41, 48
Edens, Alex. 42, 73
Edens, Alexander 21
Edmonson, Wm. 79
Edmunds, David 30, 64
Edwards, Jno. 78
Edwards, John 22
Edwards, Nicholas 40, 71
Ehney, Jno. 68
Elledge, Abrm. 62
Elledge, Isaac 62
Ellick, Fredk. 45
Ellient, Andrew D. 30
Ellient, Andw. 64
Elliott, Barnard 34, 72
Elliott, Hanard 30
Ellis, Henry 44
Ellis, Jesse 53
Ellis, William 23
Elsinore, Jas. 44
Elsinore, Kath. 67
Emerson, Wm. 80
Emery, Abrm. 62
Emmerson, Wm. 49
Emory, Robert 4
England, Charles 22
England, Chas. 76
England, Ingram 54
Entrekin, Jno. 67
Entrekin, John 22
Entrekin, Thos. 66
Ernest, John 30, 68
Erwin, Alex. 68
Eubanks, Jno. 72
Eubanks, John 22

Evans, Ezekiel 23, 56
Evans, Jabez 62
Eveleigh, Thos. 37
Faris 36
Fariss, William 23
Fariss, Wm. 73
Farmer, Wm. 41
Farrar, Field 66
Farrar, Leonard 21, 59
Farrow, Field 76
Fatheree, John 42
Faust, Jacob 24, 57
Fayssaux, Peter Dr. 34
Fayssoux, Peter 79
Fearson, Jno. 44
Feast, James 30
Feast, Jas. 72
Ferguson, Jas. 54
Fields, Jerimiah 23, 50
Filpot, John 38
Filton, Herrald 35
Findsley 36
Fitzgerrel, Ambrose 21, 48
Fitzgerrel, Garret 48
Fleming 57
Flood, Morgan 74
Forbes, Wm. 53
Forsyth, Robt. 75
Fowler, B. 60
Freeman, William Cpt. 9
Freman, Amos 55
Frenau, Peter 39, 51
French, Jos. 54
Fuller, Modica 21, 76
Fullerton, Robert 24
Fullerton, Robt. 54
Gabriel, Jno. 47
Gadsden, Philip 51
Gadsden, Thomas 30
Gadsden, Thos. 72
Gadson, Thos. 43
Gaily, Jas. 62
Gamball, James 30
Gambrall, Jno. 64
Gant, Giles 60
Garner, Thos. 21, 60, 68
Garrett, Dickison 60
Gates 40
Gellespie, Danl. 45
Gentry, David 62
George, Britain 22, 51
Gervais, Lewis 44
Gilbert, Jonathan 65
Gilder, Isaac 22, 49
Giles, Thomas 30
Giles, Thos. 36
Gilespie, Francis 76
Gilham, Jas. 71
Gillaird, Jno. 67
Gillam, Jas. 59
Gillaspie 58
Gillaspie, James 22
Gillaspie, Jas. 40

Gillaspie, Mathew 76
Gillen, Alex. 64
Gillen, Alexander 30
Gillespie, David 56
Gillespie, Mathew 57
Gillespy, Wm. 71
Gilliland, Jno. 73
Gillison, Archibald 37
Gillison, Jas. 39, 59
Glen 79
Glen, Governor 5
Glen, John 24
Glenn 59
Glenn, Bernard 59
Glenn, Spilsby 76
Glenn, William 23, 42
Glin, M. 35
Glover, Fredk. 61
Golding, Anthony 36
Goodlett, David 40
Goodwin, Chas. 67
Goodwyn, Jno. 49
Goodwyn, Uriah 30, 34
Gorget, John Francis 65
Gorly, West 32
Gotcher, John 38
Gotcher, Joshua 60
Gotcher, Wm. 60
Gottoway, Peter 65
Goucher, Henry 44
Gough, Wm. 66
Goulden, Ruber 52
Gourley, Jannet 59
Gowan, Jno. 53
Gowdy, Robert 4
Gowen, Jno. 54
Graham 39
Graham, Edw. 38
Graham, Edward 22
Graham, James 24
Graham, Mas. 74
Grant, Alex. 36
Grant, Colonel 7
Grant, Giles 73
Grant, Lodrick 4
Grant, Robt. 59
Grant, William 22
Grant, Wm. 65
Gray, Peter 34, 35
Gray, William 21
Gray, Wm. 34, 42
Grayson, Jno. 34, 39
Green, Abednego. 70
Green, Abednigo 23
Green, Aquilla 62
Green, Elisha 22, 40
Green, Henry 21, 70
Green, Jno. 59, 62, 76
Green, Robert 70
Greer, David 73
Greer, Isaiah 63
Gregory, Jonathan 76

Griffeth, Brit. 39
Griffin, Anthony 41
Grimes, Davis 41
Grimke, Jno. 63
Grimke, John F. Lt. 30
Grissum, Jno. 72, 78
Grissum, John 22
Grooms, Gilbert 30, 49
Guest, Wm. 49
Gutherie, Francis 38
Guy, William 23
Guy, Wm. 67
Hacket, James 51
Hail, Daniel 41
Hairston, Wm. 37
Hale, Abner 50
Hall, Dr. 37
Hall, John Sr. 37
Hall, Jos. Dr. 78
Hall, Joseph 37
Hall, Peter 75
Hall, Robert 70
Hall, Sam 41
Hallum 58
Hallum, Bazzel 44
Hallum, Bizzel 43
Hallum, Jno. 43, 58, 60
Hallum, Thos. 79
Hallum, Wm. 58
Hambleton, Jas. 70
Hamilton, Andw. 47
Hamilton, David, 43, 44
Hamilton, James Jr. 30
Hamilton, Jas. Jr. 79
Hamilton, Jno. 34, 45, 72, 79
Hamilton, John 21
Hamilton, Thos. 53
Hamilton, William 21
Hamilton, Wm. 43, 53
Hammenger, Jas. 45
Hammoger, Jas. 45
Hammond, Lt. Colonel 9
Hampton, Thos 65
Hampton, Wade General 9
Hampton, Wm. 47
Hand, Samuel 42
Haney, Charles 21
Haney, Chas. 64
Hanks, Ann 75
Harbin, Thos 76
Harden, Jno. 64
Harden, John 21
Harhen, Gabriel 52
Harkins, Hugh 21, 39, 61
Harkins, Walter 39, 61
Harlin, Ellis 63
Harlston, Isaac 30, 41
Harper, Bennett 79
Harper, Jno. 60
Harper, John 21, 72
Harper, Robert 37
Harper, Wm. 69, 72

Harris, Golman 38
Harris, Gustin 38
Harris, James 36
Harris, Jno. 61, 63
Harris, John 67
Harris, Stephen 78
Harrison, Jno. 34
Haston, Saml. 47
Hatton, John 4
Haulcom, Joel 54
Hawkins, Benj. 32
Hawkins, Jas. 41
Haynie, Chas. 78
Haynie, Jno. 75
Haynie, John 21
Haynie, Wm. 75
Hays, Henry 63
Hays, Jno. 78, 80
Hays, John 22, 63
Hays, Patrick 54
Heargraves, Chas. 56
Henderson, David 57
Henderson, Jas. 57
Henderson, Jos. 54
Hendricks, Moses 23, 71
Hennington, Jno. 61
Henry, John 68
Herrin, Elijah 23, 47
Herriot, Jno. 37
Hervey, Abslom 47
Hext, William Cpt. 30
Hext, Wm. 40
Hickman, Benj. 64
Hickman, Benjamin 21
Hickman, William 22
Hickman, Wm. 64
Hill 55
Hill, Henry 74
Hillhouse, Jno. 68
Hillhouse, John 22
Hodges, Wm. 52
Holden, Thos. 63
Holland, Jacob 21, 72
Holland, John 30, 77
Hollen, Wm. 61
Hollingsworth, Isaac 32
Holmes, D. 17
Hona, Wm. 68
Honey, William 21
Honey, Wm. 69
Honey, Wm. Jr. 69
Hood, Jno. 59
Hood, John 21
Hood, Richd. 74
Hook, John 4
Hooper, Enoch 54
Hopkin, David 67
Hopper, Moses 76
Horry, Peter 40
Hort, Wm. 60
Horton, Hannah 75
Horton, Isaac 73

Howard, Abraham 22, 35
Hoynie, Chas. 38
Hudson, Jno. 55
Hudson, John Sr. 22
Huger, Isaac 7
Huger, Jno. 69
Huggins, Jno. 55
Huggins, John 30
Hughes, Bernard 5
Hughes, Chas. 43
Hughes, Gen. 64
Hughes, Thos. 43
Hulom, Thos. 43
Hulom, Wm. 43
Humphrey, Jno. 48
Hunecut, Eli 37
Hunter, Henry 52, 53
Hunter, Jno. 44
Huston, James 24
Huston, Jas. 69, 70
Hutchins, Michael 48
Hutson, Geo. 73
Hutson, George 21
Hutton, Joseph 23, 37
Huxham, Wm. 66, 67
Ingram, Jas. 61
Inlow, Potter 41
Irby, Isham 22, 63
Irby, Isham 52
Irby, John 63
Irwin, Jno. 67
Irwin, Jos. 35
Isbell, Pendleton 41
Jackson, Jno. 44, 77
Jay, Aeson 47
Jeffers, Geo. 65
Jenkins, Jas. 52
Jett, James 32, 50, 63
Jett, Jas. 57
Jinkins, Thomas 39
Johnson, Abigail 52
Johnson, Jno. 47
Johnson, John 24
Johnston, Jno. 40
Johnston, Robt. 66
Joiner, Jno. 37
Jones 36
Jones, A. C. 71
Jones, Benj. 56
Jones, James 58
Jones, Lewis 35, 36, 37
Jones, Moses 22, 69, 80
Joor, Geo. 73
Joorr, Geo. 69
Jordan, Jas. 47
Jordon, David 36, 56
Jordon, James 70
Kanin 33
Kays, Maria 78
Kays, Peter 46
Keaton, Wm. 78
Keith, Alex. 65
Keith, Danl. 65

Kelley, Jno. 74
Kelley, John 4
Kelly 63
Kelson, Geo. 44
Kennady 63
Kennady, Jas. 73
Kennedy, Chas. 57
Kennedy, Jas. 35
Kennedy, William Ebenezer 56
Keysey, Levi 19
Keyton, Wm. 78
Kilgore 70
Kilgore, James 23
Kilgore, Jas. 40, 71
Kilpatrick, Alex. 33
Kilpatrick, James 23
Kilpatrick, Jas. 33
Kilpatrick, William 22
Kilpatrick, Wm. 32, 33
Kilpatricks, Jas. 33
Kirkland, Hugh 33
Lamar, Thomas 32, 33
Land, Jos. 46
Langley, Moses 69
Lantague, Anthony 4
Laurens, Henry 7
Lawrence, Benj. 59, 61
Lawrence, Jno. 34
Lawrence, William 17
Lawrence, Wm. 75
Lay, Charles 34
Lay, Francis 58
Ledbetter, Joel 23, 56
Lee, Andrew 39
Lee, Joshua 55
Leonard, Lachlin 30, 44
Leonard, Locklen 43
Leonard, Mary 43, 44
Lesley, Thos. 47
Lesley, Wm. 67
Lessly, Wm. 76
Lewis, Jno. 55
Liddle, Andrew 36, 38
Liddle, Geo. 76
Liddle, Jas. 50, 52
Lidle, George 30
Light 73
Lince, John 36
Lincoln, Jas. 67
Lindsey, Ephraim 51
Lindsey, Ephriam 43
Little, Jas. 37
Little, Wm. 33
Lofton, Saml. 55
Logan 79
Long, James 37
Long, Jas. 37
Loston, Saml. 55
Lovelady, Jno. 69
Lowdle, Robt. 76
Lowry, Henry 64
Lusk, Robt. 44

Lynch, Isaac 44
Lynch, William 42
Lyttleton, Governor 5, 6
Macky, Wm. 53
Manson, William 24
Marion, Francis 7
Marrah 59
Martain, Saml. 71
Martin 67, 80
Martin, Jas. 52, 75
Martin, Jas. Dr. 71
Martin, Jno. 43, 46, 61, 62
Martin, Joseph 37
Martin, Louis D. 80
Martin, Wm. 79
Mauldin, Blake 75
Mauldin, Jno. 78
Maverick, Lydia 50, 51, 52
Maximillian 69
Maxwell 39
Maxwell, Jno. 39
Maxwell, John 24
Maxwell, Robt. 71
May, James 4
Mayfield, Elijah 72
Mazyck, Daniel 39
Mazyck, Stephen 34
McAdoo, Jas. 56
McBain 4
McCaleb, Wm. 58
McCalep, Wm. 77
McCalip, Wm. 56
McCall, James Cpt. 9
McCambridge 64
McCane, Peter 71
McCarter, Jno. 47
McClesky, Alex. 68
McCollum, Danl. 47
McCord, John 4
McDonald, David 4
McDowall, Alex. 67
McDowd, David 5
McDowel, William 5
McDowell, Robt. 40
McGee, Jno. 49
Mcgee, John 30
McKinney 4
McLain, Alexander 24
McMahan, Jno. 58
McMillon, Danl. 57
McMurtrey, Jos. 74
McTier, William 5
Medland, Lewis 80
Merick, William 30
Merick, Wm. 79
Middleton, Robt. 50
Miles, Chas. 65
Miller 80
Miller, Eliz. 65
Miller, Francis 34
Miller, Geo. 72
Miller, Isaac 71

Miller, Jas. 66
Miller, Jno. 44
Miller, John 70
Miller, Robert 24
Miller, Wm. 65
Milligan, Jacob 30, 64
Millikin 4
Milling, Hugh 48
Mills, Gilbert 30, 47
Mills, Gilly 46
Millwee, Jas. 77
Milwee, James 37
Mitchel, Ephriam 58
Mitchell, Ephriam 61
Mitchell, Lieutenant 8
Monnow, Richard 67
Montgomery, Colonel 6
Moore 42
Moore, Alex. 66
Moore, Elial 76
Moore, J. 73
Moore, Jno. 46, 52
Moore, Thomas 30
Moore, Thos. 74
Morehead, Jno. 72
Morgan, Jerimiah 38
Morrel, Wm. 47
Morris, John 36, 37
Moss, Thos. 47
Moultrie, John 7
Moultrie, William 7
Moultrie, Wm. 80
Mountries, Alex. 75
Muleaston, Jno. 48
Mulligan, Jacob 66
Mullwee, Jas. 74
Muloster, John 32
Murphey, Edw. 37
Murphey, Edward 30
Murphree 55
Murphree, Levi 57
Murphree, Wm. 54
Nash, Reuben 64
Naylor, Geo. 50
Naylor, George 23
Neils, Wm. 66
Nevin, James 30
Nevin, Jas. 44
Nicholas, Chas. 34
Nickelson, Jno. 69
Nickles, Ambrose 68
Nixon, Alex. 34
Nixon, Alexander 30
Noble, Alex. 56
Nochelson, Ambrose 60
Nored, Saml. 66
Norris, Andw. 56
Norris, Daniel 30, 74
Norris, Patrick, 76
Norwood, Jno. 42
Norwood, Saml. 52
O'Brian, Dennes 34

Oatwell, Wm. 70
Occonostota 6
Oliphant, David 60, 66
Oliver, Alex. 36, 37, 38
Owen, John 36, 37
Owens, Jno. 37
Owens, Richard 15
Page, Jno. 66
Pairson, Jno. 67
Parker, Jno. 47, 56
Parsons, Jno. 61
Parsons, Major 32, 49, 64
Parsons, William 30
Parsons, Wm. 47
Patterson 59
Patterson, Jas. 38
Patterson, Jno. 68
Paucet, Faila 32
Peacock, Robt. 46
Pearis, Richard 3
Pearis, Richard Cpt. 8
Pearson, Henry 36, 47
Peircy, John 38
Peirson, Henry 35
Pendleton, Henry 20
Percell, Henry Rev. 79
Perkins, Peter 42
Perkins, Solomon 33
Perry, Benj. 57
Perry, Nat. 56
Perry, Nathl. 56
Person, Harry 43
Pewet, Fields 61
Philips, Jacob 22
Phillips, Jacob 50
Philpot, Jno. 41
Pickens, And. 45
Pickens, Andrew 7, 19, 44
Pickens, Andw. 61, 76
Pickens, Ezekiel 71
Pickens, Gen. 62
Pickens, Mr. 16
Pickens, Robert 77
Pickens, Wm. 62
Pickens, Wm. Gabriel 57
Pilgrim, Ezekiel 50
Pinckney, Charles Cotesworth 19
Pinckney, Chas. 69
Pinckney, Gen. 51
Pinkston, Obidiah 78
Plunket, Charley 41
Plunkett, Charley 22
Pollard, Richard 30, 79
Ponder, Jas. 75
Porter, Jas. 66
Porter, Philip 66
Portman, Jno. 61, 62
Potter, Thos. 54
Powers, Alex. 52
Prator, Philip 22, 70
Price, Elijah 79
Price, Ensign 15
Purcell, H. Rev. 79

Ramsay, Jos. H. 47
Ramsey, Thos. 68
Ranfrow, Wm. 62
Rany, Benj. 73
Read, Wm. 59
Reed, Geo. 75
Reed, Jacob 60
Reed, Jos. 62, 64
Reed, Wm. 61, 73
Reid, George 38
Reid, Hugh 70
Reighty, Wm. 42
Rhyny, Ann van 77
Rice 72
Rice, Jas. 72
Richards, William 22
Richards, Wm. 77
Richardson, Colonel 8
Richardson, Jno. 74
Riddle, William 30
Riddle, Wm. 79
Ridgeway, Saml. 80
Riggs, Widow 66
Right, Adam 50
Rigway 79
Robberd 33
Roberts 73
Roberts, Richard 30, 62
Roberts, Zeph. 58
Roberts, Zephimah 58
Robertson, James 30
Robertson, Jas. 70
Robertson, Jno. 50, 53
Robeson, Alex. 51
Robinson, David 72
Robinson, Eliz. 53
Robinson, Jno. Jr. 51
Robison, Jno. 48, 75
Robuck, Geo. 53
Rolston, Lewis 48
Rose, Hugh 58
Ross, Andw. 65
Ross, Jas. 67
Rowe, Andw. 52
Rowland 58
Russell, Thomas 30
Russell, Thos. C. 34, 79
Rutherford, General 10
Rutherford, James 22
Rutherford, Jas. 65
Rutledge, President 9
Ryley, Wm. 42
Sadler 57
Sadler, Richard 60
Salamon, Bryan 4
Salmon 54
Sargeant, Wm. 38
Saxon, Chas. 51
Saxon, Jas. 35
Saxon, Joshua 46
Scarff, Jos. 44
Scarff, Joseph 30

Scott, James 30, 70, 74
Scott, Robt. 38
Scott, William 30
Scott, Wm. 34
Searight, Wm. 47
Self, Presly 41
Selfridge, Robt. 74
Seys, Chas. 44
Shadden, David 47
Shankling 76
Sheinger 33
Shilton, Lewis 48
Shirley, Jas. 65, 67
Shoaler, Geo. 76
Shubrick, Thomas 30
Shubrick, Thos. 40
Sidle, Geo. 62
Silman 55
Simkins, Arthur 19
Simmons, Jno. 50
Simon 49
Simpson, Jas. 47
Simpson, Reuben 22, 56
Simpson, Wm. 45
Sinkler, Peter 43, 44
Skelton, Jno. 56
Skelton, John 30
Sloan, David 22, 62
Sloan, Wm. 32
Slwenston, Robt. 74
Smith 52
Smith, Aaron 30, 47, 48
Smith, Benj. 51
Smith, Chas. 58
Smith, David 51, 52
Smith, Jacob 39
Smith, James 49
Smith, Jno. 46, 49
Smith, John 47
Smith, Jos. 54
Smith, Joseph 70
Smith, Ralph 66
Smith, Richard 4
Smith, Robt. 64
Smith, Saml. 60, 61, 75
Smith, Wm. 69
Smithson, Albert F. 49
Snell, Alex. 38
Speed, Robert 33
Spence, John 34
Spence, Robert 30
Spence, Robt. 65
Spencer, John 30
Springer, Jno. 34
St. Marie, Levacher 40
St. Marie, Levacher de 30
Starrett, Benj. 35
Steel, Charles 38
Steel, Isaac 46, 47
Steele, Abner 51
Steele, Wm. 42
Step, Jos. 57

Stephen 53
Stephen, Wm. 69
Stephenson 56
Stevens, Mashack 50
Stewart, Benj. 40
Stewart, Robt. 66
Stewart, Thos. 53
Stokes, Shadk. 77
Stone, Prichard 39
Strange, Stephen 74
Stuart, Adam 67
Stuart, Henry 8
Stuart, John Cpt. 8
Sullivan, Wm. 64
Sunn, Frederick, Dr. 30
Sunn, Fredr. Dr. 40
Swift, Wm. 45
Swords, Jno. 58
Tate, Jas. Sr. 57
Tate, Robt. 57
Tate, Wm. 59
Taylor, Polly 65
Taylor, Saml. 49, 61, 62, 63
Tenison, Jno. 53
Tennant, William Rev. 16
Terrel, Aaron 48
Terrel, Henry 49
Thacker, Martin 76
Thomas, Amanatious 50
Thomas, John 24
Thompson, James 24
Thompson, Wm. 32, 55, 56
Thomson, Jas. 78
Tile, Reuben 42
Titsworth, Isaac 44
Todd, James 60
Tolbert, Saml. 79
Tombien, Moses 69
Tuble, Elijah 39
Tumage, Jno. 73
Turner 36
Turner, Eleaser 30
Turner, Eleazer 71
Turner, Joshua 75
Turner, Wm. 65
Turpin 38, 50
Twilly, Jno. 62
Twitty, Wm. 33
Uriah, Capt. Goodwyn 34
Vance, Jacob 58
Vanderhort, Major 42
Verner, Jno. 62
Verner, Sarah 62
Waddel, Robert 34
Waddle, James 30
Waddle, Jas. 44
Wade 57
Wade, David 74
Wadsworth, Benj. 51
Wadsworth, Stephen 50, 51
Wadsworth, Susannah 51
Wadsworth, Thos. 46, 50, 51

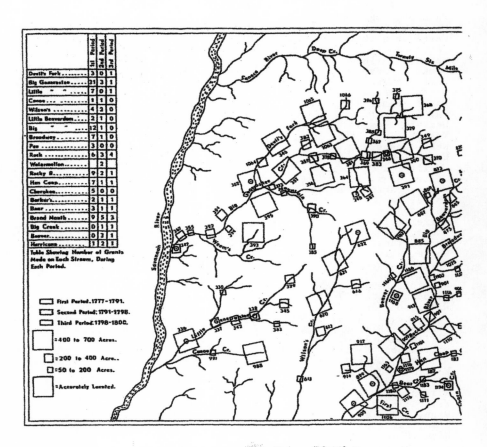

	1st Period	2nd Period	3rd Period
Devil's Fork	3	0	1
Big Generation	31	3	1
Little "	7	0	1
Canoe	1	1	0
Wilson's	4	2	0
Little Beaverdam	2	1	0
Big " "....	12	1	0
Broadway	7	1	0
Pen	3	0	0
Rock	6	3	4
Watermelon........		2	
Rocky B.	9	2	1
Hen Coop..........	7	1	1
Cherokee..........	5	0	0
Barker's..........	2	1	1
Bear	3	1	1
Broad Mouth	9	5	3
Big Creek	0	1	1
Beaver..............	0	3	1
Harricane	1	2	1

Table Showing Number of Grants Made on Each Stream, During Each Period.

☐ First Period.1777-1791.
☐ Second Period: 1791-1798.
☐ Third Period: 1798-1800.

☐ =400 to 700 Acres.
☐ =200 to 400 Acres.
☐ =50 to 200 Acres.

☒ =Accurately Located.

No. 1a - Lower Pendleton District

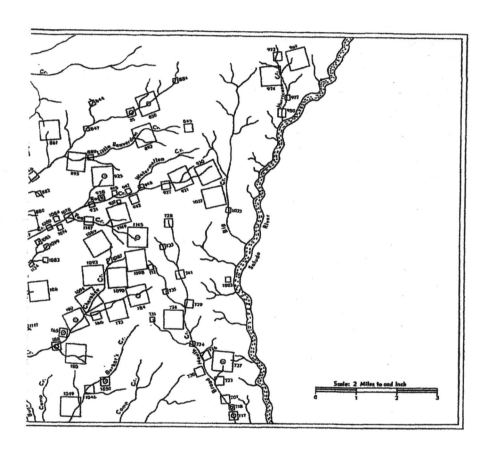

No. 1b - Lower Pendleton District

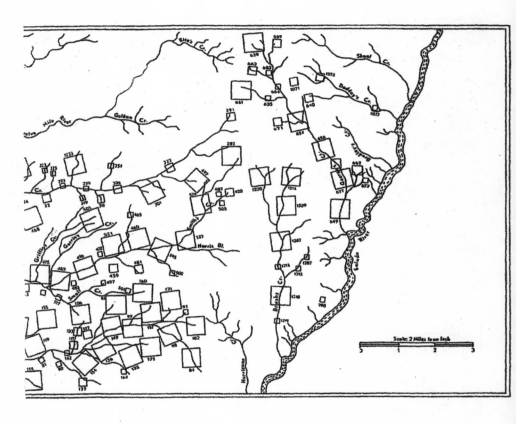

No. 2b - Seneca River and Main Tributaries

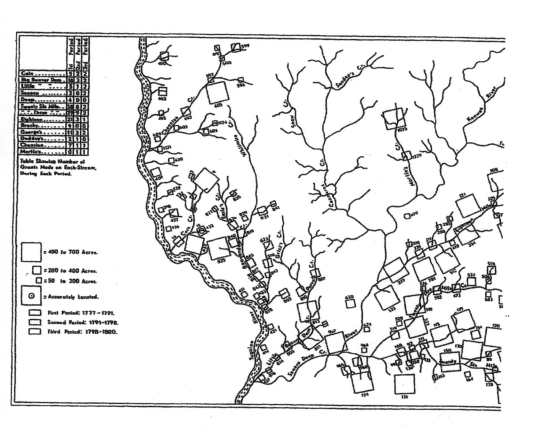

No. 2a – Seneca River and Main Tributaries

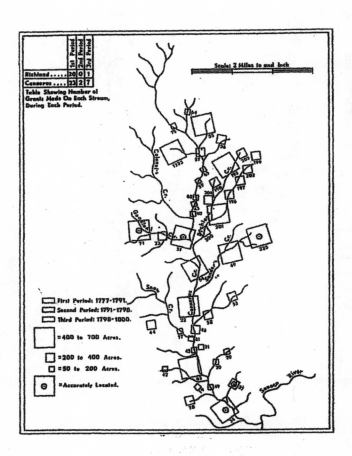

No. 3 - Coneross

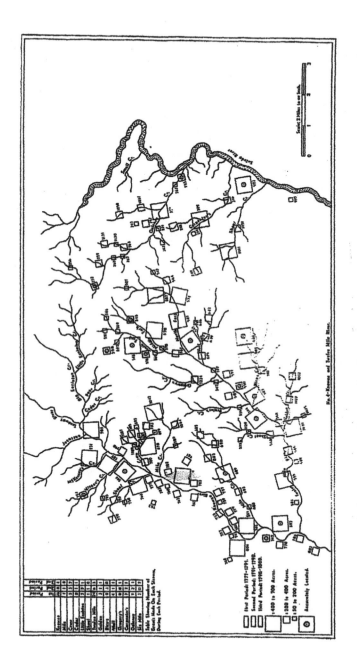

No. 4 - Keowee and Twelve Mile Creek

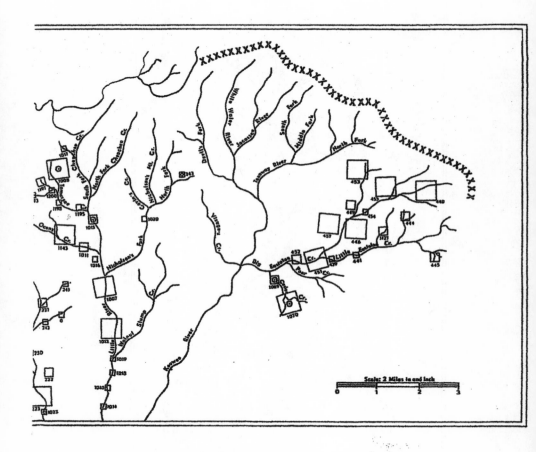

No. 5b - Upper Pendleton District

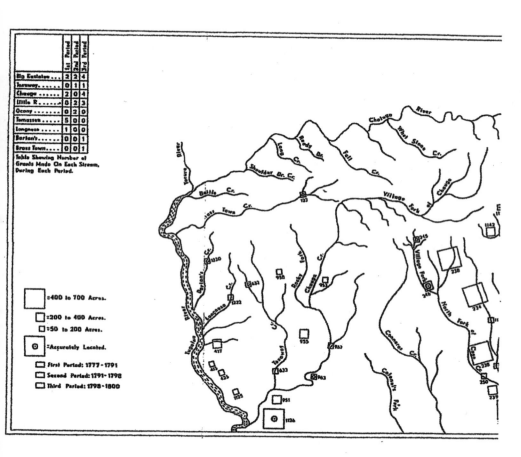

	1st Period	2nd Period	3rd Period
Big Eastaton ...	2	2	4
Toxaway	0	1	1
Chauga	2	0	4
Little R.	0	2	3
Ocony	0	2	0
Tomassee	5	0	0
Longnose	1	0	0
Barton's	0	0	1
Brass Town....	0	0	1

Table Showing Number of
Grants Made On Each Stream,
During Each Period.

=400 to 700 Acres.

=200 to 400 Acres.

=50 to 200 Acres.

=Accurately Located.

First Period: 1777-1791

Second Period: 1791-1798

Third Period: 1798-1800

No. 5a - Upper Pendleton District